8 STEP CONFIDENCE CRASH COURSE

Hardie Grant

BOOKS

DOMONIQUE BERTOLUCCI

8 STEP CONFIDENCE CRASH COURSE

FEEL GOOD ABOUT WHO YOU ARE
and THE LIFE YOU LIVE

Published in 2023 by Hardie Grant Books, an imprint of Hardie Grant Publishing

Hardie Grant Books (Melbourne)
Wurundjeri Country
Building 1, 658 Church Street
Richmond, Victoria 3121

Hardie Grant Books (London)
5th & 6th Floors
52–54 Southwark Street
London SE1 1UN

hardiegrant.com/au/books

A catalogue record for this book is available from the National Library of Australia

8 Step Confidence Crash Course: Feel good about who you are and the life you live
ISBN 978 1 74379 868 3

10 9 8 7 6 5 4 3 2 1

Publisher: Pam Brewster
Project Editor: Elena Callcott
Editor: Allison Hiew
Design Manager: Kristin Thomas
Designer: Regine Abos
Typesetter: Celia Mance
Production Manager: Todd Rechner
Production Coordinator: Jessica Harvie

Colour reproduction by Splitting Image Colour Studio
Printed in China by Leo Paper Products LTD.

Hardie Grant acknowledges the Traditional Owners of the country on which we work, the Wurundjeri people of the Kulin nation and the Gadigal people of the Eora nation, and recognises their continuing connection to the land, waters and culture. We pay our respects to their Elders past and present.

For Sophia and Tobias

✴

So many people are looking outside of themselves
for ways to feel good on the inside.
They think that they'll feel confident
and start believing in themselves
when they've done this, got that or look a certain way.

But your confidence shouldn't be dependent
on the goals you have achieved or the things you've done.
It's not about your dress size, the number on your bathroom scales
or the balance on your bank statement.
And your sense of self-belief shouldn't need compliments,
positive feedback from others,
or a whole lot of likes from people you barely know.

But if the way you think and feel about yourself
isn't based on what you've got, what you've done,
or what other people think or say about you,
where does it come from and what can you do
so that you can feel good about yourself and your life?

The answer lies in your mindset:
the set of thoughts you hold about yourself and your life.

You deserve to feel good about who you are and the life you live –
and when you get your mindset right you will.

CONTENTS

A NOTE FROM DOMONIQUE ...

When I started out as a life coach, my work was all about setting and achieving goals. But over the years I've realised that there is something *even more* important than achieving your goals ... feeling good about yourself *regardless*.

In this book, I'm going to give you a crash course on the simple things you can do to boost your confidence and build your self-belief.

I'll explain all the changes you can make to the way you think, feel and act so that confidence and self-belief start to come much more naturally and easily to you. And by the end of this book, you're going to know exactly what you need to do to feel good about who you are, and the life you live.

In the 'about the author' page at the back of this book, you will read about the other books I've written, the podcasts I've hosted and the client work that I do. But my life hasn't just been one big career highlight reel. Like everyone, I've had my fair share of highs and lows, and ups and downs – and I'll tell you about some of them in this book. But through it all, I've learned that, win or lose, triumph or fall flat on my face, it won't change anything about who I am or how I feel about myself.

My successes don't make me a better person and my failures don't make me a worse one.

I've learned to feel confident in who I am – to feel good

about myself – and to know that I am enough … regardless of what is, or isn't, going on in my life.

And that is what I want the *8 Step Confidence Crash Course* to do for you.

I'm going to show you how to boost your confidence, build your self-belief and ultimately change the way you feel about who you are and the life you live.

Once you know how to feel good about yourself, everything will start to feel easier for you. Plus, you'll be able to catch yourself as soon as you start to enter a negative confidence spiral, and know exactly what you need to do to get your thoughts and feelings back on track.

Now although this is a crash course, it doesn't mean it's always going to be easy. Some parts of our time together, the things you'll learn or the ideas I'll share, might make you a little uncomfortable. It might make you think about things in ways you're not used to, or encourage you to face up to certain challenges, negative thoughts or unhelpful behaviour patterns once and for all. If this happens, please don't tune out or mentally press fast forward. Instead, sit with your feelings and see what you can learn from them – what insights or lessons do they hold?

You need to get comfortable with discomfort if you want to live your best, most brilliant life.

It will always be easier to live an ordinary life – most people are fine with 'fine' and okay with their life being 'okay', but if you want to live a happy and fulfilling life, it's important that you're not. But you've chosen to read this book, so I don't think I need to remind you of that. I'm guessing that you're here because you're ready to feel good about who you are and the life you live – not just someday, but every day.

Let's get started …

WELCOME TO THE 8 STEPS

STEP 1: GIVE UP PERFECTION

To begin, I'll explain why you are good enough just as you are and how your flaws are just the flip side of your strengths. By the end of this chapter, you'll know how to accept your imperfections as a part of who you are, what to do when you mess up or make a mistake, and what you need to focus on instead.

STEP 2: DO YOUR BEST

Then you'll learn how to turn jealousy into inspiration and how to encourage yourself when things feel tough. By the end of this chapter, you'll understand the difference between doing your best and needing to be the best, and why your goals aren't your only path to success.

STEP 3: IMPRESS YOURSELF

In this step, you're going to learn how to protect your self-worth like the valuable asset it is, instead of carelessly throwing it away. By the end of this chapter, not only will you have shifted your focus away from your flaws, you'll know why failure is often the fastest route to success, and how to make sure that it doesn't mess with your head.

STEP 4: EXPECT GOOD THINGS

It's up to you to make good things happen, and in this step you'll learn how to take ownership of your life to give yourself the best chance of success. By the end of this chapter, you'll know the difference between assessing the worst-case scenario and worrying incessantly, and you'll know what to do with your thoughts instead.

STEP 5: CHEER YOURSELF ON

Instead of being your own worst enemy, become your biggest fan and learn the right way to lift yourself up when you fall down. By the end of this chapter, you'll know how to ignore your inner critic, what to do when you feel anxious or scared, and how to set each day up for success.

STEP 6: RISE TO THE CHALLENGE

Not everything in life is going to run smoothly and so in this step I'll explain why you should never try to squash your fears and how to confidently handle whatever life sends your way. By the end of this chapter, you'll know why you need to step out of your comfort zone, how to ask for the respect you deserve, and when to put your needs first.

STEP 7: SHINE YOUR LIGHT

No one can make you feel unworthy without your permission, so in this chapter I'll teach you how to let go of the past, take back control of the dimmer switch and turn up the light in your life. I'll show you how to work out what you really want, and what changes when you embrace a brighter future and take charge of your life.

STEP 8: FALL IN LOVE WITH YOURSELF

The most important relationship you will ever have is with yourself, and in this step you'll learn how to show yourself some love. By the end of this chapter, you'll know how to respect your boundaries, forgive your failings and, ultimately, be the star in the love story that is your life.

As you read each chapter, I'd love to know what your biggest insights and your favourite mindset shifts have been. You can find me on Instagram or Facebook @domoniquebertolucci – I can't wait to hear your thoughts.

Throughout this book, I'll be sharing a range of tips, strategies and suggestions to help you boost your confidence and build your self-belief. To help you put everything you're learning into action I've created a workbook that contains the key lessons from each chapter, plus some exercises and journal prompts to help you to put each lesson into practise.

The workbook is free, and you can download it as a PDF from domoniquebertolucci.com/confidence-crash-course.

STEP 1:

GIVE UP PERFECTION

Realise that you're perfectly imperfect and accept your imperfections as a part of who you are.

Everybody makes mistakes, so don't let yours define you or undermine you. You are good enough just as you are and your flaws are just the flip side of your strengths.

I think of myself as a recovering perfectionist.

When I was younger, being the Type A/straight A kind of person I was, I easily fell into the habit of trying to be perfect at anything and everything I did. Not only was this a pressured way to live, it also put me on a fast track to burnout and played a big role in a horrible time in my life – my quarter-life crisis!

From the outside, you wouldn't have necessarily thought that I was a perfectionist. I had a zigzag start to my career that began with modelling, tip-toed through fragrance counters and beauty halls, and led to me working in the high-flying world of banking before I found my way to the coaching, consulting and training I do today. But even though I was marching to the beat of my own drum, I was still holding on to those drumsticks way too tightly; I had unrealistic expectations for myself and my life, and when I messed up, as we all inevitably do, I was a champion at beating myself up over it.

During that quarter-life crisis – when I realised that although my life looked good on paper, it felt hollow and empty to me – I remember sitting in my therapist's office, crying my eyes out and saying, 'I know there is a big lesson in this for me, but I wish I could hurry up and learn it!' Even when it came to learning my lessons the hard way, I was putting myself under pressure to do it perfectly!

Eventually, the lessons did come to me, and I learned so many things from that time in my life. One of the most important was to finally give up both the conscious and subconscious ideas I had about being perfect.

I learned that no matter how hard I tried I would make mistakes and get things wrong; that even when I did get things right, they still might not turn out the way I wanted them to or lead me to the outcome I'd been working towards; and that while some things would look right at the time, in hindsight they might turn out to be completely wrong for me.

I learned that gaining weight didn't make me a failure any more than being slim meant that I was a success; that being loved didn't mean I was in love; and that no matter how committed I was, some friendships wouldn't stand the test of time.

At the end of it all, I learned that life was messy. And that if I wanted to thrive – to feel good about who I was and the life I was living – I would need to stop trying to be perfect and to embrace my life as it was, in all its imperfect glory.

STOP TRYING TO BE PERFECT

If you want to boost your confidence and build your self-belief the first thing you need to do is accept that perfection is impossible to achieve. Nobody can be perfect, not even you.

Perfection is an unachievable goal.

There might be things you want to change, improve, or get better at, and that's okay.

I'm not going to try to talk you out of your 'continual improvement plan' (at least not yet). But even if your list of improvements is a mile long, I want you to know that you are already good enough, just as you are.

✳✳✳

✻ YOU ARE ✻ GOOD ENOUGH

If you want to feel good about who you are and the life you live you need to be willing to accept yourself just as you are – 'warts and all' as the old saying goes. Although you might not be like an old crone from a Grimm Brothers' tale, and warts may not be at the top of your list of things to worry about, if you're like most people you probably *do* have a list of faults and imperfections that you've been keeping track of – a list that has been eroding your confidence.

You are enough.

Regardless of whether these perceived flaws are keeping you up at night, or quietly nagging away at you during the day, learning to accept yourself alongside them or in spite of them is fundamental to building your confidence and changing the way you feel about yourself for the better. Even if your list of improvements is a mile long, I want you to know that you are already good enough, just as you are.

✴ YOU CAN ACCEPT YOURSELF ✴ and CONTINUE TO IMPROVE

Like any change, making the mindset shift to self-acceptance isn't always easy, or instant. For most people, the idea of accepting your imperfections, while sounding good in principle, doesn't come with the instant sense of relief that they always hope it will. Instead, whether it's an individual client or a group of people in a workshop, I regularly watch people squirm, both physically and metaphorically, as they consider letting go of all the different ways they have been criticising themselves and putting themselves down. Sooner or later someone always pipes up and asks, 'Does that mean you are telling me to just put up with things as they are and to stop trying to improve myself or my life?'

Absolutely not! As a coach, I always want you to focus on being the best you can be. But people misunderstand this as an invitation to make a long list of all the different ways they could and should try to be better, and then beat themselves up for having such a long list. But just because there are things you could do to improve yourself doesn't mean that you are not good enough just as you are. These are not mutually exclusive ideas. You can accept yourself as you are, *and* you can make plans to improve or change. The key here is not to wait *until* you've made those improvements before you accept yourself.

Accepting your imperfections doesn't mean that you won't ever do anything about them. It just means that you are not going to think less of yourself until you do.

✳ FORGIVE YOUR ✳ MISTAKES

Although it might feel like we've begun by ripping the Band-Aid off with these uncomfortable truths about perfectionism and how it erodes your confidence and self-belief, what I want you to do next is to give yourself a break and be a whole lot kinder and easier on yourself … especially when you do make a mistake or mess up in some way.

I want you to accept that you're human.

When you make a mistake, it's okay to feel bad about it, but that doesn't mean that you need to feel bad about yourself. Although you've made a mistake, the person that you are doesn't change just because you've made it; making a mistake is about what you've done, not who you are.

Everybody makes mistakes.
Don't let yours define you or undermine you.

You can still look for ways to improve, learn your lessons and apologise if you need to.

But you don't need to beat yourself up or engage in endless self-criticism to motivate yourself to make sure you don't make the same mistake again. Making yourself feel bad won't fix things or make them better … but accepting your mistake and forgiving yourself will make *you* feel a whole lot better.

CARLA'S CONFIDENCE CRASH COURSE

To be honest, I found the lessons in Step 1: Give up perfection a bit confronting.

I've always thought of myself as a positive, motivated person. I know I'm a bit of a Type A personality … I work hard, I like to get things right and I always try to do my best. But Step 1 really got me thinking.

I've realised that I haven't been trying to do my best – I've been trying to be perfect. I always thought being a perfectionist was a good thing – when people described me that way I took it as a compliment! But I can see that was maybe a bit misguided and I've been putting myself under all this pressure to get everything right, all of the time.

It wasn't until I started to think about how exacting I am about everything that I realised how exhausting it is. Both physically AND emotionally. From the way I look to the work I do, our home and everything I surround myself with … I never cut myself any slack. Everything has always has to be 'perfect'.

And it hasn't been working. The truth is, it never has. Instead of feeling good because of how hard I try, I feel bad about myself because something always slips. Nothing I do ever feels quite good enough.

And that's not even the worst part. I can see now that my perfectionism hasn't just been ruining my confidence, it's had an impact on other people's too. My husband and my two teenage daughters complain that I'm always criticising them and that nothing they do is ever good enough in my eyes.

It's definitely time to change. I've realised that perfection is a lost cause. No one is perfect – I've got to stop expecting it from myself and the people around me.

Being a perfectionist is exhausting and I'm ready to try another way. From now on, I'm going to be a lot more accepting of myself … and everyone else!

✳ RECOGNISE THE FLIP SIDE ✳ OF YOUR FLAWS

While making a mistake might be a one-off incident, your flaws are the less-than-perfect parts of you, parts of you that are likely to make an appearance again and again. Instead of berating yourself or criticising yourself for these perceived flaws, I want you to learn to accept them with love and grace.

You are perfectly imperfect.

So often, the things we think of as flaws are actually the flip side of one of our more positive qualities – a quality we might not want to give up. If you want to feel good about yourself, you need to make the decision to recognise that your 'flaws' – the flip sides to your strengths – are a part of who you are too.

As a natural extrovert, I'm talkative and outgoing. The upside of that is that if you meet me at a party or event where you don't know anyone, I'll strike up a conversation and introduce you to everyone I know. The flaw, or flip side, to this quality is that sometimes I take up more than my fair share of airtime in a conversation. We'll be at dinner with friends, and I'll be excitedly talking about something, and I'll feel my husband gently (or firmly) tap me on the knee – his discreet way of reminding me that it's time to give someone else a turn to hold the floor. I could focus on this as a flaw – 'sometimes I talk too much'. Instead, I'd rather see being talkative and outgoing as a quality that gives me plenty of advantages, but also has a flip side that I need to be mindful of.

Instead of viewing yourself as a set of isolated qualities, see yourself as a whole person. One with a whole lot of strengths and a few not-so-strong points too. I want you to know that not only is that okay … it's a perfectly imperfect way to be.

✻ STOP CRITICISING YOURSELF ✻

If you are always trying to be perfect and then criticising yourself when you're not, the only thing you're doing perfectly is chipping away at your confidence and undermining your self-belief.

~~~

Self-criticism is a symptom of perfectionism.

The first step to changing any behaviour is to acknowledge it, so pay extra attention when you criticise yourself to see if you can identify what perfectionist ideal you are buying into. Be interested in your thoughts; observe them. See what insights they hold or what patterns you can discover. But instead of judging yourself or berating yourself for having them, pay attention to what initiated or triggered this self-criticism and what you could do next time to cut this negative thought spiral off before it has the chance to begin.

Once you've become more aware of your perfectionist behaviour and of the self-criticism that follows, you can begin to think about breaking this unhelpful habit and replacing it with a new, more encouraging one instead. Think of it like changing the song or playlist on your favourite music app. If you want to stop playing the heart-thumping music that you've been exercising to and start listening to some chill-out music to unwind with, you simply select a different track.

For example, whenever I drop something, make a mistake or mess up in some largely inconsequential way, instead of saying, 'I'm such an idiot', 'Geez, you're so stupid', 'I can't believe you did that again', I simply apologise if I need to, and remind myself that I'm good at other things. I actually say that to myself – sometimes out loud. 'I'm good at other things.'

When I say that, I'm not bragging or big-noting myself or telling myself I'm it-and-a-bit. I'm simply reminding myself that while I might have failed at this thing, there are plenty of things I've succeeded at.

Listening to your inner critic – that voice in your head that is picking away at your faults and putting you down for being anything less than perfect – is like any other unhelpful habit. You might have been doing it a long time, and it might take a bit of effort, but it's a habit you can break.

✳ CHOOSE HAPPINESS ✳ OVER PERFECTION

For all this talk about giving up the pursuit of perfection, I want to reassure you that you still can focus on being good at some things. In fact, you still get to be *great* at lots of things. Overcoming perfectionism isn't about giving up your passions or the things you care about doing well. It's about having reasonable expectations of yourself for the things that are important in your life and appropriate expectations for the things that aren't.

It's about saying no to being the perfect parent, the perfect employee, the perfect boss or the perfect partner. It's about not trying to have the perfect body, perfect home or perfect Instagram feed. At the same time, it's about knowing that you can still give your best to these and all the other things that really matter to you.

If you strive for perfection,
you'll never be happy.
But if you focus on being happy,
you won't care about being perfect.

KEY INSIGHTS

STEP 1: GIVE UP PERFECTION

1. Perfection is impossible to achieve – nobody can be perfect, not even you.
2. You are good enough just as you are.
3. You can accept yourself as you are *and* make plans to improve or change.
4. Everybody makes mistakes. Don't let yours define you or undermine you.
5. Your flaws are the flip side of your strengths – you are perfectly imperfect.
6. Self-criticism is a symptom of perfectionism. Don't engage in it
7. Instead of chastising yourself, encourage yourself.
8. Perfectionism and happiness cannot coexist – choose to be happy, not perfect.

JOURNAL PROMPTS

1. Think of a mistake you have made that you are still berating or chastising yourself over. Make a note of the lessons you have learned from this mistake and acknowledge how much wiser you are as a result of it.
2. Make a list of the flip side or positive qualities of each of your perceived flaws. Next to each item make a note of how that quality serves you or works to your advantage.
3. Think about the self-critical thoughts that play on repeat in your head. Make a note of a new thought you can replace them with and make a commitment to letting this thought be the one that you default to from now on.

STEP 2:

DO YOUR BEST

Understand the difference between doing your best and needing to be the best, and why your goals aren't the only path to success.

There is no need to compete in the game of life. Turn jealousy into inspiration and encourage yourself when things feel tough. There will always be someone who has more or who has done more, so focus on your intentions instead.

Growing up, I was proud to be a 'Nipper', as junior surf lifesavers are called in Australia. Every Sunday I went down to the beach and competed in all kinds of surf and sand events. The ocean swim was always my favourite, and I was regularly the first girl across the line at my club. But as someone who can't run three feet without twisting her ankle, I was always last in the sand sprints – and don't even get me started on what happened when I tried to paddle fast on a board. It was like a comedy sketch … at least it was for everyone else. But win or lose, every week I'd head to the club with a big smile on my face. Of course, as a competitor I wanted to do my best, but my best was always measured against someone else's – and in my case, there was *often* someone else who was better.

But my biggest victory as a nipper didn't happen in the ocean or on the sand. At the age of twelve, I won the Club Man Award, the sportsmanship award given to the person who most embodied the spirit of the club. I knew it was a big deal. For a start, it was called Club *Man* because a girl had never won it before. (It was renamed the Club *Person* Award the following year.) But, as well as being a win for girl-kind, this award underlined one of the principles I have always tried to live by.

I can still feel the warm glow of pride I felt during the award ceremony when the presenter said: 'When Domonique crosses the line first in the swim she smiles from ear to ear ... and when she crawls across the line last in the sand sprint she is smiling just as hard. Win or lose she is doing her best, and she is smiling and enjoying herself while she does it.'

Do your best and enjoy yourself while you do it. If you take that approach, you will always feel good about yourself and your life.

✳ DON'T COMPETE ✳

The very first thing I want you to do, to focus on being your best, is to stop competing – or at least stop competing against anyone and everyone else. There are, of course, exceptions to this. But even if you are an Olympic athlete or engaged in another activity where winning does mean everything, you still don't need to be competitive in any other aspect of your life.

*There is a big difference
between doing your best
and needing to be the best.*

You don't need to compete to have the biggest house, the largest bank balance or the smallest waist. You don't need to be the one with the highest achieving children, the best job title or the most likes on social media. Because there is no winning this competition – there will always be someone who has more or who has done more.

Instead of trying to be *the best*, I want you to take the time to work out what being *your best* means – and then I want you to make that your focus point from now on.

✷ GET INSPIRED ✷

Although I've just asked you to stop competing or comparing yourself to other people, I realise that you're probably not going to suddenly become blind to people who are doing better than you, have more than you, have achieved goals you're still striving for, or have done things you haven't found the time for, and that's okay.

The fact that you are noticing what other people are doing doesn't have to be a problem for your self-confidence if you can channel these observations into a source of inspiration instead of material for self-flagellation. Instead of putting yourself down for what you *haven't* done or criticising yourself for what you *haven't* got, be inspired by the fact that you now have proof of what is possible – of what can be done and of what can be achieved.

If someone else is doing it or having it,
it proves that it is possible for you, too.

This is the power of your mindset in action: switching your thoughts from those that deflate you, and make you feel less than or not good enough, to thoughts that lift you, inspire you and remind you of what is possible. By changing your thoughts in this way, you'll change the way you feel – from inadequate and deflated to motivated and uplifted – which will make it so much easier to take any action you need in order to do, be or have all of the things you're feeling inspired about.

✳ BE OBJECTIVE ✳

When you're feeling envious it's much harder to recognise the effort and commitment that has gone into someone else's success, as well as the sacrifices or compromises they may have had to make along the way.

Once you've started viewing other people's successes, achievements and accomplishments as a source of inspiration instead of one of envy, you will also find that it's much easier to be objective about how much work it took to get what they've got or do what they've done. That might leave you feeling more motivated than ever, or you might find that you're not as inspired as you thought you would be.

Be objective about the effort that goes into success,
instead of just focusing on what comes out of it.

Every now and then, I find myself feeling envious of someone who has completed their PhD. I just love the sound of those letters and I'd be lying if I said I've never imagined them coming after my name. But if I switch my focus from envy to inspiration, something immediately shifts inside me – I remember how much work goes into a PhD, how many years it takes, and all the research it involves.

My shoulders relax, I exhale and I go back to being happy with the path I have chosen ... and being comfortable in the knowledge that the only way I am ever likely to end up with a PhD is if I'm awarded an honorary one!

✳ MANAGE ✳
YOUR ENERGY

Now that you know to not compete with other people or waste your energy feeling envious, I want you to shift your attention to the things you *do* need to focus on. There are a finite number of hours in the day, days in the week, weeks in the year and years in a lifetime, so it's important to be smart about where you put your energy so that you work towards the things that matter most to you in life.

Being busy for busy's sake is not doing your best. Doing your best is not about throwing yourself at any and every situation to prove that you've got what it takes, and it's not trying to do everything or be everything for everyone else, either.

When you make a commitment to doing your best,
you also need to make a conscious decision about
what that best is going to look like.

Doing your best is about being intentional about the amount of effort you commit to any given situation. It's about being aware of what you want to put in *and* what you want and need to get out of it.

STEVEN'S CONFIDENCE CRASH COURSE

I've always been very competitive. In my role at work, it's a pretty important attribute because we're always measured on our performance. I want my team to win … and I want to win. My career depends on it and so does my bonus!

But Step 2: Do your best made me see that I've let this approach spill over into the rest of my life – and what works in sales doesn't necessarily work at barbecues or any other part of my social life.

I realise now that I've fallen into the habit of needing to win at everything – and when there hasn't been anything specific to compete over, I've been channelling my competitive nature into needing to be right. What might start off as friendly jostling can quickly become heated if I feel like I'm losing a debate or someone else is getting one better than me. And I'm at my worst when I feel jealous of someone else's success or if they have something I want.

I feel a bit embarrassed now that I realise I've been behaving this way. I really had myself convinced that it was all a bit of fun, but I can see now that my desire to win has probably left the person I've been sparring with feeling like they're losing … and no one wants to feel like they're losing when they're out having beers or enjoying a meal with friends.

From now on, I'm going to be a lot more aware that the only place I need to compete is work and that I need to park this approach in the other areas of my life.

And if I find myself feeling triggered by someone else's victory – by something they've got or done – I'm going to take a step back. Rather than being jealous of their success and allowing that to bring out the worst in me, I'm going to choose to be inspired instead.

✳ THINK BIG, ✳
BUT AIM SMALL

Being intentional about your efforts also means having reasonable expectations about when, where and how you are able to apply those efforts. This is not about being complacent about your life or trying to do as little as possible, but if you want to boost your confidence you need to make sure that you don't set yourself up for failure before you begin by having unreasonable expectations of the amount of available time, money or energy you have.

I'm a coach and so you've probably been expecting me to tell you to aim big, reach for the stars and set as many Big Hairy Audacious Goals, or 'BHAGs' as some people call them, as possible. But that's not what I think at all. I want you to think big – to know that anything you want is possible and that nothing is impossible – but I want you to aim *small*.

Whatever your hopes, dreams and ambitions are, if you want to build your confidence and build your self-belief, the answer isn't to aim high, take a giant leap and fall flat on your face. The idea is to aim high, work out what your best effort looks like and take small but consistent steps – steps that you know you can maintain for as long as it's going to take to get there.

~~~

Aim high, build a good ladder
and climb it step by steady step.

The more successful you feel, the more successful you'll become, so even though this slow and steady approach might not sound that exciting, each of those little wins – every step you take on your ladder – is going to leave you feeling good about yourself and the progress you're making.

✳ SET YOURSELF ✳
UP FOR SUCCESS

While you're ditching your BHAGs, I want you to consider parking a lot of your other goals too, at least for the time being. From a young age, we are told that we need to set goals and achieve them if we want to live a happy and successful life. But most people fail to achieve their goals most of the time, and it doesn't feel good. When that happens, you blame yourself for lacking motivation, commitment or staying power. But I've got a different take on all this. I think the problem lies with the nature of goals themselves: how we set them, when we set them and why we set them. I believe the whole goal-setting process you've been taught is inherently flawed.

I want to be clear here. I am not anti-goal, but the success/ failure rollercoaster that goes with them … I'm not such a fan. I think that we all need to shift our focus away from thinking that goals are the be-all and end-all and put them back in their rightful place – as just one of the many tools we have available to help us get what we want.

The majority of the time when we set SMART goals – which stands for Specific, Measurable, Achievable, Realistic (or as some have updated it to, Relatable) and Time-Based goals – they are simply a 'best guess' of what is possible. And yet, we hold ourselves accountable to them as if our success was guaranteed and the only explanation for ever failing is because we weren't good enough.

Nothing kills confidence like
feeling like you're not good enough.

✳ FOCUS ON YOUR ✳ DESTINATION

While achieving your goals can be motivating in the short term, failing to achieve your goals is demotivating in equal measure. But if you're not going to set goals, or at least not set them as often, you're probably wondering what you should do when you want to confidently move forward or make progress in your life. The answer is to think more broadly and set clear intentions: your big picture, the thing that all of your individual goals are working towards.

Setting intentions doesn't have to be complicated – it can be as simple as asking yourself, 'What do I want to say and how do I want to feel about … ?' and then listening closely to your answer. For example, your goal might be to lose 5 kg. There is a whole range of intentions a goal like this could be supporting. Your intention might be to improve your health, fit into your clothes again or eliminate unhealthy eating habits.

Why does this matter? If you're moving closer to your goal, who cares what mindset work is going on behind the scenes, right? Wrong! The honest answer is, when everything is going according to plan and you are on track, it might not matter quite as much. But how often does everything in life go according to plan and turn out exactly the way you want? Not that often in my experience. For most people, trying to make progress in any area of their life will be a mix of ups and downs. Highs and lows. Successes and, you guessed it, failures.

*Don't set yourself up for failure
before you even begin.*

When things are running smoothly, it's much easier to maintain the right mindset. But having the right mindset or foundation for the things you are working towards will mean that when you *do* hit a bump in the road, it will be much less likely to send you completely off track. When you focus on your intentions and something doesn't turn out according to plan, you can adjust your plan or switch to a different approach while keeping your eyes on the destination you want to reach.

By focusing on your intentions, what you really want to achieve will become clearer. You'll feel much more confident about pursuing it and stay completely committed to the inspired, motivated actions you need to take to get it, regardless of any highs or lows you experience along the way. (I'm so passionate about this approach, this shift from goals to intentions, that I created a whole process around it called the Intention Method™ and I've started training other people in it too!)

It's times like this when you will be glad you took the time to create a solid foundation for success and that you focused your efforts on your overall intentions rather than on a single specific goal.

✳ DECIDE WHAT YOUR ✳ BEST LOOKS LIKE

Now that you're not feeling quite so hung up on your goals – especially the ones you haven't achieved – you will be free to consciously decide what your best does and doesn't look like. When you're no longer setting yourself up for failure by trying to do the impossible, you will feel much more confident about where to apply your attention and your efforts, and why it matters.

Decide where and when you want to give your best, and don't worry about the rest.

Taking this approach will also give you a much clearer idea about the things that aren't important. And instead of pushing yourself to be the best at things you don't care about, you'll be able to confidently say to yourself 'It really doesn't matter' and know that you genuinely mean it.

KEY
INSIGHTS

STEP 2: DO YOUR BEST

1. Instead of trying to be the best, just focus on being *your* best.
2. Be inspired by other people's success, not jealous of it.
3. Before you envy someone's success, appreciate what it has taken to get it.
4. Be intentional about the effort you put in and what you hope to get out.
5. Think big, but aim small.
6. There is a time and a place for your goals – it's just not all of the time.
7. Focus on your intentions and keep your eyes on your destination.
8. You get to decide what your best does – and doesn't – look like.

JOURNAL PROMPTS

1. Create an *inspiration and aspiration* list of all the people whose success inspires you, excites you and reminds you that the things that you want from life are possible.

2. Make a note of any areas of your life where you have been giving your best, but that on reflection really don't warrant that level of effort. Take a minute to get clear on what a reasonable level of effort is for each of these areas and make the decision to give this much, and only this much, from now on.

3. Think of a goal you have been struggling to achieve, something you've been on the success/failure roller coaster with, and make a note of the intention or big-picture idea that this goal is supporting. Pay attention to how this shifts the way you feel about your goal and make the decision to focus your attention on your intention from this point on.

STEP 3:

IMPRESS YOURSELF

Protect your self-worth like the valuable asset it is, instead of carelessly throwing it away.

Failure is often the fastest route to success so shift your focus away from your flaws, learn your lessons, dust yourself off and don't let it mess with your head.

One day, the store manager of one of my favourite clothing brands – where I used to browse regularly and buy occasionally – told me that the company was hosting a cocktail party so that their best customers could meet the founder and designer, and that she had added my name to the guest list. How exciting! I put the date in my calendar and waited for the official invitation with all the event details to arrive.

Except that it didn't. Nothing by post, nothing by email, not even a phone call. I was so disappointed. But at the same time, it made sense to me. The company must've had hundreds of customers who didn't wait until the sales before they bought, and who spent much more money in the store than I ever did. My name must've been on a list of *potential* guests and I just hadn't made the cut.

I was back browsing in the store a week or so after the event, and the manager asked if I'd enjoyed meeting the designer. 'Oh, I didn't go,' I said. She looked surprised, so I quickly explained that I'd never received an invitation. 'What do you mean,' she said – '*I* invited you.' So, I shared my assumption about why I hadn't made the final guest list. 'Not at all,' she explained. Each store had only submitted five names. There had only been 50 people invited to the event and I'd been one of them.

But, it wasn't until she asked her next question that I realised what had really happened … and why I had missed out on attending this event. 'Why didn't you tell me that your invitation hadn't arrived?' she asked. I felt my cheeks suddenly burn hot, and in that moment I released that, without even knowing I had done it, when my invitation hadn't arrived, I'd decided that it was because *I wasn't good enough.* Sure, the specifics in this instance were that 'I wasn't a good enough customer … ' but that felt like it was just a detail. This core feeling, of not being worthy, of not being enough, was the one making my cheeks burn.

It turns out there had been a typo in my email address – a simple admin error. If I had felt good enough and worthy of attending this event, I would have let the manager know that my invitation hadn't arrived and asked if she could investigate it for me. The problem would have been resolved and this Cinderella would have gone to the ball.

✳ EXERCISE YOUR ✳ SELF-BELIEF

While the 'event that never was' took place several years ago, this experience has stayed with me. After all, I'm a coach: I do confidence and self-worth for a living.

If you'd asked me before that day, I would have told you that my self-belief was unshakeable. I've since come to realise that self-belief is like fitness – not only do you need to keep exercising it to maintain it but, in the same way you can be running fit but not swimming fit, cycling fit but not stair fit, you need to think about overall fitness and not just the specifics.

*Your self-belief can be strong
in one area while still needing
to be developed or nurtured in another.*

If you want to feel good about who you are and the life you live you need to pay attention – not only to those times when you feel great about yourself but also to experiences like the one I just described, where you realise that you and your self-belief have a little work to do. Only when you've identified areas where your self-belief isn't as strong as you would like it to be can you then start to exercise it, and build it up.

✳ YOU ARE A WORK ✳
IN PROGRESS

That feeling I described – that feeling of not being good enough – is like kryptonite to your self-confidence. If you're not paying attention and you don't catch it as soon as it appears, it can quickly poison the way you feel not just about other parts of your life, but about yourself. It's like taking an express elevator from 'I'm not good enough at this or that' to 'I'm not good enough. Full stop.'

So instead, I want to take a lesson from the Silicon Valley playbook and think about it the same way software company or app developer talks about their products. Just because you've found things you need to improve doesn't mean you're not good enough. When they put out a new program or app, they know it's not perfect, and they're fully aware that it still has some faults in it. But they release it to the world knowing that it is good enough for now, and then they get back to work creating an even better version for the future.

You are good enough right now,
even if the next version of you
is going to be even better.

And this is how I want you to start thinking of yourself. You might be version 28 or 33, 46, 54 or whatever your current age, and I'm sure there are plenty of things you'd like to improve – you are, and always will be, a work in progress. But that doesn't mean that the current version of you isn't good enough. It just means that the next version will be even better.

✳ FAILURE IS A PART ✳ OF THE JOURNEY

Fear of failure is one of the biggest things that holds people back from living their best possible lives. They become too afraid to take a risk – too afraid to even try – in case they fail. They worry about the embarrassment of getting it wrong, the discomfort of seeing their idea flop, the pain of missing out, or of being forced to accept defeat. But while embarrassment, discomfort and emotional pain might feel horrible in the moment, these feelings won't kill you. And they don't last.

I've worked with lots of founders and entrepreneurs over the years, and in the start-up community there is a popular expression that captures what I believe is the best cure for the fear of failure. Fail fast.

Instead of worrying if you've got it right and holding yourself back until you can be 100 per cent certain that you have, founders and entrepreneurs push themselves to get their ideas into the market as quickly as possible. Even if their business idea or new tech venture is a failure, they want it to hurry up and fail so they can learn their lessons, dust themselves off and start all over again.

✳ Have a go.
✳ Learn your lessons.
✳ Dust yourself off.
✳ Try again.

∿∿

Whenever you catch yourself feeling afraid of failing,
challenge yourself to have a go.

You don't need to be an entrepreneur or the head of a start-up to put this empowering process into action – it works just as well for everyday challenges too. If it works out on the first attempt, brilliant. But if not, learn your lessons, dust yourself off and try again … and then keep following this formula until you succeed.

BE WILLING TO FAIL FABULOUSLY

On the flip side of failing faster lies one of the most powerful coaching questions of all – 'What would you do if you knew you couldn't fail?' I can still remember the cascade of emotions I felt when my first coach asked me that question more than 20 years ago. It is such a simple question. And it is so powerful.

What would you do
if you knew you couldn't fail?

If you remove the risk of failure – the risk of disappointment, embarrassment and other uncomfortable or painful feelings – from the equation, what would *you* be willing to take a chance on? Did a light bulb go off for you when you read that? Did you get goosebumps or a flash of clarity? After all these years working as a coach, I still get a shiver of excitement every time I ask myself that question.

The point of this question isn't to promise you a failure-free life, but to remind you how restrictive or even debilitating the fear of failure can be, and how much we hold ourselves back when we try to avoid that risk. I would much rather fail at something that I was excited about – something that mattered to me – than hold myself back, play it safe and wonder about *what could have been.*

I call this failing fabulously.

It's not that I want to fail and it's certainly not that I like failing – I feel disappointment, embarrassment and pain just as much as the next person – but I decided long ago that I would much rather fail fabulously than succeed at mediocrity.

DON'T LIVE IN FEAR

One of my favourite quotes of all time comes from the Baz Luhrmann movie *Strictly Ballroom:* 'A life lived in fear is a life half lived.' I don't want to half live my life and I'm sure you don't want to, either.

Instead of avoiding failure,
focus on where and
how you want to succeed.

What gets you up in the morning? What gets you excited or puts a smile on your face? And, when your time in this life is done, what is it that you want to make sure you tried so that you can say, *at least I gave it a go*?

If you want to live a happy and fulfilling life, a full and interesting life, a rich and rewarding life, you need to stop wasting energy avoiding failure and focus your attention on where and how you want to be a success.

CAROLYN'S CONFIDENCE
CRASH COURSE

I've been playing it safe for so long, I'd stopped noticing that I was even doing it.

When I was 28, I cashed in my life savings and started a leisurewear company. Things got off to a great start – my designs were featured in magazines and online. I was pretty excited about it all. I had a strong creative vision, but it became clear that I really didn't know enough about running a business. So while there was money coming in the door, there was even more going out.

I was so busy trying to grow my brand and reach for the stars that I didn't notice the landslide forming underneath me.

I had two crazy, exciting years, and then it all came crashing down. I lost everything I put into that business. But worst of all, I totally lost my confidence.

My savings were gone and I still had bills to pay, so I got a job on the design team for a big, but very dull, clothing company. It was a long way from my vision, but it paid well and it gave me a chance to catch my breath.

And for a little while, safe, steady and secure was just what I needed. But that was nearly ten years ago …

When I first got this job, I told myself it would be for a year or two: just enough time to pay back my debts, save some money and start all over again. But I felt like such a failure and the weight of it clung to me.

I realise now, after Step 3: Impress yourself, that I was feeding that 'failure' feeling over and over. I was focusing on my mistakes instead of looking at all the things I had achieved and learned during that experience.

So I've decided that I've been licking my wounds for long enough. What doesn't kill you does make you stronger and I'm going to start designing for myself again. I don't know how things will turn out, but I've learned so much and I'm ready to stop hiding away and start believing in myself again.

It's better to fail fabulously than to succeed at mediocrity – I'm definitely making that my mantra from now on.

✳ ACKNOWLEDGE YOUR ✳
POSITIVE QUALITIES

Most people find it easy to create a big, long list of all the ways they could improve and all the things about themselves that they should change. And maybe you're no different. But what about all the things that are already good about you – all the things you get right, all your positive qualities, and all the ways you already do your best, give your best and try your best? How quickly could you produce that list? If you're like most people, you'd probably find it difficult – not because these things don't exist, but because they're not at the top of your mind.

If you want to give your confidence a big boost, create a list of all the things that are already great about you – and don't just keep this list in your head. Write down all your strengths, positive qualities and things that you are pleased with or proud of and keep that list close to hand, so that you can find it and read it over whenever your confidence needs a boost. Some of my favourite places for storing this list are the notes section of your phone, the front page of your journal or inside your wardrobe door.

Let's go back for a moment, to the example I gave earlier about Silicon Valley. When a company releases a new version of one of their products into the market, they already have a list of all the enhancements and improvements they are planning to make in the next version … but this is not what they lead their marketing messaging with.

They don't make excuses for why it isn't perfect or tell you about how much better they still want it to be. They simply focus on all the features and benefits of the current version. And this is the approach I want you to take, too. Instead of keeping your tweaks, adjustments and improvements front and centre, I want you to keep your 'what's great about me right now' list at the top of your mind, even if you know exactly what you're planning to improve in the next version.

There is nothing wrong with wanting to continue to improve or upgrade to a better version of you. Just don't make these the details you focus on.

✳ CELEBRATE YOUR ✳ STRENGTHS

So many people are afraid to express their talents in words or actions. They're worried that talking about them will make them seem big-headed and they're worried that using them will make the people around them feel intimidated or uncomfortable.

Hiding your light,
your strengths and your talents,
from the world doesn't serve you.

I'm not suggesting you write your talents in the sky or take out a billboard and use it as a 60-foot résumé, but I want you to stop ignoring them or denying that they exist. Take your list out and read it regularly – say it out loud so that you get comfortable hearing yourself talk about your strengths and talents in your own voice. Speak of them in the first person: say 'I am' and 'I have' and 'I do … '.

Celebrate your strengths and talents. Get comfortable owning them, confident talking about them and ready to use them, and don't ever hide them or apologise for having them.

✹ FOCUS ON YOUR ✹ TRUE WORTH

Your worth is not determined by the number on your bathroom scales or the balance of your bank account. Your worth is not a reflection of how many likes your posts get, how many people you know or what car you drive.

Your self-worth is determined by how you feel about your*self*.

No one can tell you how to feel about yourself –
that's something you, and only you, get to decide.

It doesn't matter what anyone else says about you – their criticisms and judgements are about them, not you. It doesn't matter what mistakes you've made or lessons you've had to learn the hard way. And I hope you know by now that it doesn't matter if there are improvements you'd like to make. All that matters is that you decide that you are good enough and that *you're worth it.*

KEY
INSIGHTS

STEP 3: IMPRESS YOURSELF

1. Your self-belief is like your fitness – it needs exercise to stay strong.
2. You are, and always will be, a work in progress.
3. Fail fast – learn your lessons, dust yourself off and try again until you succeed.
4. It is better to fail fabulously than succeed at mediocrity.
5. Instead of avoiding failure, focus on where and how you want to succeed.
6. Make a list of your positive qualities – keep it close to hand and top of mind.
7. Instead of hiding your strengths and talents, celebrate them.
8. Your self-worth is defined by how you feel about your*self*.

JOURNAL PROMPTS

1. Make a list of the areas where your self-belief is strongest and make a note of one thing you can do in each of those areas to challenge yourself and keep your self-belief strong.

2. Answer the question, 'What would I do if I knew I couldn't fail?' and make your answer as rich and detailed as possible. When you've finished, identify all the different ways you can take one step closer to this vision.

3. Make a list of all your strengths, positive qualities, and the things you are most proud of. Keep this list somewhere where you can see it easily and read it (or even better, recite it out loud) at least once a day.

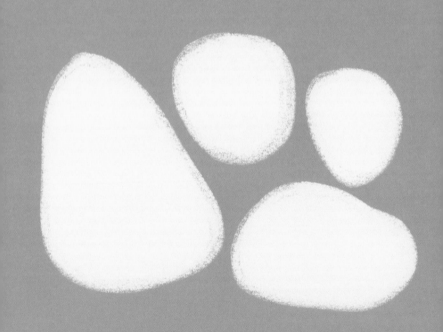

STEP 4:

EXPECT GOOD THINGS

Take responsibility for your life and give yourself the best chance of success.

It's up to you to make good things happen, so master your mindset, take ownership of your life and give yourself the best chance of success.

When I first left my corporate career and began working in personal development, one of my boldest dreams was to have my own television show. YouTube hadn't taken off at that time and none of the social media platforms that let you share your thoughts with the world existed yet. So if you wanted to get your message out to a wide audience, TV was the best way to do it.

I had several promising meetings over the years and, although they never led to that dream becoming my reality, it was one of those 'promising' meetings that taught me one of the most important, confidence-boosting lessons of my life.

I decided it was time to visit Los Angeles and see if I could develop some of my industry contacts into a tangible opportunity. Although I was planning to meet with an agent who worked at a small firm, I wanted to aim higher and so I sent off a meeting request to a Big Shot Agent too. The answer came back: Yes! He would meet with me.

Having a TV show might never have been one of your dreams, so it's quite possible you have no idea how much of a big deal this was. So you're just going to have to trust me when I tell you, this was BIG. I mean, BIGGER THAN BIG. This meeting felt like it could be the doorway to everything I had been dreaming about. Except, it wasn't.

The meeting was cancelled, rescheduled, cancelled, and rescheduled again. On my last day in LA, I finally got a call saying that the assistant-to-the-assistant of the big shot agent would meet with me – but only if I could come to the office right now. I raced across town but the meeting was a disaster! Not only did the assistant's assistant have zero interest in me or my ideas, but I was allergic to something in the office and had a coughing fit so bad that I was sure they were getting ready to dial 911.

I arrived back home to a bank balance that was thousands of dollars lighter and a short, polite email from the agent that pretty much said, 'Don't call us, we'll call you', which we all know means 'we won't be calling'.

But after the initial bruising of my ego healed, I noticed something unexpected about the aftereffects of the whole experience. Rather than this debacle of a trip eroding my confidence and making me feel bad about myself, it fuelled my self-belief. I didn't get an agent, sign a contract or turn that particular dream into a reality. But I'd backed myself and given it 100 per cent, and the confidence boost that gave me made the trip worth every cent.

✳ BE INTENTIONAL ✳
ABOUT YOUR LIFE

The reason why this experience was ultimately confidence-building and not crushing was because by going after my dream – win or lose – I had taken ownership of my life. Instead of playing the 'let's see what happens' game and letting my life just drift along, I had been intentional about what I wanted to create.

It is your life and you get to decide
what kind of life you want it to be.

The very first thing I want you to do as you learn to expect good things is to be intentional about your life and commit to being the one who makes 'good things' happen for you. Being intentional about your life doesn't mean that you can suddenly control everything – but so many people drift along in life and then wonder why it feels like nothing ever turns out the way that they want it to. Drifting along in life won't necessarily lead to an unhappy or unpleasant life any more than drifting along in a sailboat will guarantee you crash on the rocks. But without any navigation – a clear intention about where you want to end up – you could end up on the rocks, you might go around in circles, or simply not move very far from where you started.

Being intentional about your life doesn't mean you need a detailed plan, precise coordinates, or a list of 101 goals you want to achieve. To be honest, I often think that's the last thing you need. As I mentioned earlier, when I'm working on intentions with my clients I always ask them, 'What do you want to be able to say – and how do you want to feel – about who you are and the life you live?' It's a big, broad question.

When you answer this question and define clear intentions for your life (or for any aspect of it) you are setting your personal true north: the direction you want your inner compass to lead you towards. If you are clear about what you're navigating towards and the overall journey you want to take, any detours along the way won't take you too far off course.

✳ STOP WORRYING ✳

Once you've set your personal true north, I want you to stop worrying about it. In fact, I want you to stop worrying about everything else, too. Most people expend way too much energy worrying about everything that could go wrong in their life.

No amount of churning and burning about what 'could' happen will ever affect the outcome; will ever affect what does happen. But worrying about things that could go wrong occupies your thoughts: you send a clear message to your subconscious that you *expect* things to go wrong.

Worrying won't change anything …
except how you feel.

Engaging in negative expectations – worrying – not only changes how you feel about the situation, it changes the way you feel about yourself. Now, you might be thinking that the way you feel is just how you feel and that it's really hard to change the way that you feel, but it doesn't have to be that way. Your feelings don't exist in isolation. They're a direct result of the thoughts you have. It's your thoughts that determine your feelings, not the other way around – and you can choose thoughts that build you up or thoughts that tear you down.

To put it another way, if you want to feel good about who you are and the life you live, it's your mindset that matters most.

And when you get your mindset right, everything else will fall will into place. Your thoughts create your feelings, and when you worry and continuously think about all the things that could go wrong you fuel feelings of fear, inadequacy and futility … just to name a few.

Instead of worrying about something that might happen (but also might *not* happen) when you *expect good things* you are able to generate a whole range of different feelings. When you have an optimistic expectation, you will find that you are much more likely to feel strong, confident, reassured and even peaceful about your future.

✻ CHOOSE YOUR ✻ THOUGHTS

Now before we go any further, I want to clear up a common misconception about worrying – or rather, not-worrying. Making the decision not to worry doesn't mean you need to be naïve to the risks of a situation or deluded about reality.

Choosing not to worry is not about ignoring a situation – it's about where you decide to focus your thoughts, mental energy and attention.

As a non-worrier (seriously, I can count on one hand the number of times I've felt worried in the last year) I am not in denial about what could go wrong. It's just not what I'm focusing on. Because it's not what I'm thinking about, the fears and anxieties that go with worrying don't take up any room in my head or steal any energy from my life.

When you consciously choose your thoughts and decide what you want to think about and how you want to think about it, you can generate feelings that make you feel optimistic, rather than overwhelmed by your life. You don't need to put your head in the sand. You can still consider the worst-case scenario if you acknowledge objectively how likely (or unlikely) it is to happen.

Consciously choose thoughts that make you feel good about the future.

I'm going to talk more about how and when you should explore the worst-case scenario in a moment, but for now, I just want you to know that when you choose not to worry, you can still acknowledge what might go wrong while focusing your energy and attention on expecting things to go right.

OLIVIA'S CONFIDENCE CRASH COURSE

People who don't know me very well would say I seem pretty confident. In my job, I have to give presentations and I know how to speak in front of a crowd. So yes, when it comes to things like that I am confident.

But while I feel confident about the things I can do, like public speaking, I don't always feel confident in who I am. I am a worrier and I'm always second-guessing myself. I know I spend way too much time thinking about the worst-case scenario – but not in a productive way like Domonique described.

When I get in that headspace, it's 100 per cent counter-productive. I think about how bad things could turn out and before I know it, I can't think about anything else. It's all bad.

Before Step 4: Expect good things, I'd never really thought about how this way of thinking affects my confidence. But now I can see that worrying about everything going wrong, doubting my decisions and feeling bad about myself are closely related.

When I think about the ways I constantly churn things over in my head it's a wonder I can think straight at all. But it's time for that to stop. I've got to stop.

I'm going to take the lessons from Step 4 and remind myself that worrying won't change anything except how I feel about myself. If my brain can quickly go from 'this could happen' to 'this is *going* to happen' when I think about the worst-case scenario, there's no reason why I can't train it to do the same thing with my *best*-case scenario.

From now on I'm going to pay a *lot* more attention to the thoughts I have so that I can choose ones that make me feel calm and confident, and I'm going to ditch the thought cycles that make me feel stressed out, anxious and just plain bad.

✳ BE CONFIDENT IN ✳ YOUR DECISIONS

While we're talking about worrying, or more importantly, not-worrying – I want you to stop worrying about getting things wrong or making the wrong decisions. When it comes to making decisions, I am a firm believer that the only wrong decision is indecision. As long as you consider your options, and consciously make a decision based on the information available, you *will* have made the right decision.

Down the track or at some point in the future different information might become available – and there is nothing like putting on a pair of hindsight goggles to see how you could have done things differently. But even if in retrospect you no longer think your decision was the best one, that still doesn't mean that you got it wrong at the time. It just means that what was the right decision, back when you made it, hasn't stood the test of time.

*Everything looks different
in the rear-view mirror.*

Stop agonising about getting it wrong and instead make the make the best decision you can right now, by focusing on the things you can see: the things that are in front of you.

Consider your options. Make a decision. And trust that the decision you have made is the right decision for you, right now.

This simple act of faith – of trusting yourself to make the right decision – will naturally give your confidence a boost, and as your confidence grows it will become easier and easier to trust yourself.

✳ HAVE A GROWTH MINDSET ✳

But, no matter how good you get at trusting yourself, there will still be lessons to learn and things that don't turn out the way you want them to, so the next thing I want you to do is get good at asking yourself, 'What will I do differently *next* time?' without judging yourself or criticising yourself for what you did *this* time.

Being able to look at a situation without judgement –
without criticising yourself or putting yourself down –
will open your eyes to so much wisdom.

When all you focus on is what you've done wrong or the mistakes you've made, you invite yourself to enter a negative spiral of self-criticism, blame or shame, and invariably take your confidence and self-belief down with it. But when you're able to take a neutral perspective and, instead of focusing on what you did wrong, focus on what you will do *differently* next time, you're activating your growth mindset.

Unless you are sleepwalking through your life, there will always be opportunities to learn and grow, so learn your lessons in a way that builds your confidence instead of tearing it down.

✴ DISCOVER YOUR OPTIONS ✴

But what about that worst-case scenario? I know the title of this chapter is Expect Good Things, but sometimes one of the most helpful things you can do for your self-confidence is to take a moment to understand your worst-case scenario – and then to know, without a doubt, you would be able to survive it.

I remember many years ago having a conversation with a client of mine who was a real worrier. Let's call him Stuart. Stuart was the CEO of a large non-profit organisation that, among other things, provided food for the homeless. Stuart was contemplating moving to a different organisation but found himself worrying about all the different ways it could go wrong. What if he wasn't successful, what if he was fired, what if he couldn't get another job, and so on.

Instead of trying to get him to switch his focus and think more positively, I kept asking ' … and what is the worst thing that could happen after that?' I can still remember the way he looked at me – like his coach had gone completely mad by asking him to be more negative, not less – but he was on a roll, so on and on he went. 'I could use up all my savings … we could lose the house, we could become penniless, homeless …' and then he broke into a huge smile.

'And then I could ask the meal truck to bring me my dinner … I mean, the guys all know me, don't they!'

By exploring his worst-case scenario in this way – all the way to its most extreme point – Stuart could see both how improbable it was that things would ever get that bad and that he could survive if they did.

Exploring the worst-case scenario
will allow you to see all the opportunities
you have to stop it from ever happening.

It was highly unlikely that Stuart's worst-case scenario would ever unfold. And I'm guessing that it's unlikely that your worst-case scenario would ever come to be, either. In most cases when you explore not just your worst-case scenario, but the pathway to it, you will be able to see all the different opportunities you have to course-correct along the way if it turns out that things aren't going the way you had hoped.

Rather than undermining your confidence, when you do it the right way, exploring the worst-case scenario can boost your belief in yourself and in your ability to adjust your plan or handle whatever may come your way.

✳ BALANCE YOUR ✳ EXPECTATIONS

There is a big difference between focusing on and expecting good things and assuming that things will always be this way. Not only will you make mistakes, get things wrong and have plenty of those lovely lessons that we already talked about, but sometimes things just won't turn out the way you want them to, through no fault of your own.

When that happens, you will have two choices you can make. Drop your bundle, give up or give in … *or*, pick yourself up, dust yourself off and get back on track again.

It is inevitable that there will be bumps along the road.
What matters is how you navigate them.

When you can balance your expectation for things to turn out well with your acknowledgement that not every outcome is within your control, you will be able to navigate your journey with more grace and greater ease, instead of giving up as soon as things don't go according to plan.

✴ FOCUS YOUR ATTENTION ✴
ON YOUR INTENTION

Once you've allowed yourself to fully explore your worst-case scenario, and acknowledge that bumps along the road are all but guaranteed, I want you to shift your focus and attention to your intention: your best-case scenario. And, with the energy you've saved by not worrying, agonising or blaming yourself, you will be ready to do all that you can to make that best-case scenario – or something that closely resembles it – your reality.

Focusing your thoughts,
feelings and energy on the things
you want to happen will give you
the best chance of making them happen.

When you *expect good things*, you give yourself a much better chance of getting them. It's not because your expectations act like a magic wand – although metaphysicists and magicians all tell me that they do – it's because by focusing your attention – your thoughts – on what you *do* want to happen, it will *feel* much more possible.

That feeling – that confident and empowered feeling – will make taking the actions that you need to make it your reality come much more naturally and easily to you.

And if focusing on what you want to happen and *expecting* good things invites The Universe to come to the party and contribute to your success … well I say, even better!

KEY
INSIGHTS

STEP 4: EXPECT GOOD THINGS

1. Be intentional about your life – commit to making good things happen for you.
2. Remember, worrying won't change anything except how you feel.
3. Consciously choose thoughts that make you feel optimistic.
4. The only wrong decision is indecision.
5. Activate a growth mindset – ask yourself, 'What will I do differently next time?'
6. Understand the worst-case scenario but appreciate how improbable it is.
7. When things don't turn out, pick yourself up, dust yourself off and try again.
8. Focus your attention on your intention – expect things to turn out well.

*

JOURNAL
PROMPTS

1. Make a list of all the things you are currently worrying about. Next to each item indicate whether it is something you can do something about or something you need to accept. If your worry is something you can influence, make a note of the action you plan to take. If it is beyond your control, make the decision to accept it.

2. Craft positive thoughts or affirmations that describe your expectations for the future, writing them in the present tense as if they have already occurred. Repeat this for any anything that you find yourself worrying about and from now on make these new thoughts the ones that are on repeat in your head.

3. Think of a decision you have made in the past that, with the wisdom of hindsight, turned out not to serve you as well as you would have hoped. Make a note about what you have learned from this experience and what you will do differently next time.

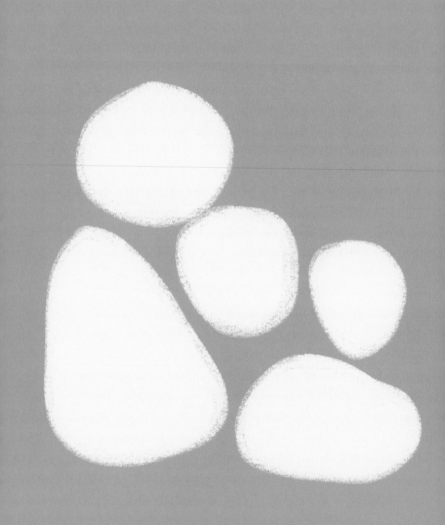

STEP 5:

CHEER YOURSELF ON

Become your biggest fan and learn the right way to lift yourself up when you fall down.

Instead of being your own worst enemy, when you feel anxious or scared, ignore your inner critic and act like your best friend would instead.

Not so long ago, I was walking my son to school and my normally cheerful and chatty little boy was tired, grumpy and out of sorts. As we walked along, I looked up at the clear, bright Sydney sky and could see that a skywriting plane had started to write a message in the blue. The plane began with a T ... and then an O appeared, and I jokingly said to my son, whose name is Toby, 'Maybe he's writing your name!'

'Really?' he said, with the wide-eyed wonder of the seven-year-old he was at the time. Given this was the first smile I had seen all morning, I decided to keep it up. 'It could be ... ' I said in my best 'I'm not giving any secrets away' voice.

As the next letter formed and took the shape of a 'B' I racked my brain to think of all the things that start with 'TOB' that this plane could be promoting, but I got stumped after Toblerone. We both stood still, craning our necks, staring up at the sky ... and sure enough, the next letter was a 'Y'.

'Mum! Mum! The plane wrote Toby!' my son exclaimed with delight. We kept watching the sky, neither of us caring if we were a few minutes late to school. But just when we thought the morning couldn't get any better the second word became clear …

R.U.L.E.S.

The plane had written 'Toby Rules' across the sky.

'Well, what do you say about that?' I asked my son.

'I think today is going to be a great day, Mum.' And he smiled from ear to ear. He squeezed my hand and raced off to meet his classmates, with his smile back to full voltage and the funk of the morning long forgotten.

You'll be relieved to know that the message behind this story isn't that the next time you are having a bad day, you need to invest thousands of dollars in a skywriter to cheer yourself up. But it does serve as a powerful reminder that how we think changes how we feel – and that a few simple words are often all it takes.

✳ BECOME YOUR ✳ OWN BIGGEST FAN

The good news is that you don't need to wait for a skywriter! If you want to bring out the best in yourself, you just need to be your own cheerleader – your own biggest fan. Unfortunately, this doesn't come naturally to most people. After spending childhood being told not to boast, brag or big-note yourself and adulthood watching tall poppies getting chopped down to size, the idea that you should be cheering yourself to success can take some getting used to.

Bring out the best in yourself
by learning to cheer yourself on.

Most people are *so much* better at criticising themselves and tearing themselves down than they could even dream of being at building themselves up. And so the very first thing I want you to focus on as you learn to be your own cheerleader is silencing your 'inner critic'.

Your inner critic is that nasty little voice inside your head that is always judging you, criticising you or putting you down. It's a mean voice that you would never dream of using on anyone else, and yet, for most people, it is chattering away in their minds so incessantly that they have stopped noticing that it is even there.

Sometimes there can be a grain of truth in what your inner critic has to say – just like a bully, it will zero in on your weaknesses, vulnerabilities, past failures, or the things you are afraid of or feeling insecure about. While evaluating your efforts and looking for the lessons learned can be a positive thing – highlighting ways you can improve or grow – your inner critic isn't nearly so discerning or thoughtful in its approach.

IGNORE YOUR INNER CRITIC

Like any bully, your inner critic is fuelled by how much attention it gets. The more you try to do battle with your inner critic, get into a debate with it or argue with it, the more likely it is to double down on its efforts to undermine you and put you down.

And just as a bully in real life gets their power from feeling like they are winning if their intended victim starts to cower or hide away in shame, nothing will fuel your inner critic more than listening to its messages and taking them to heart – than letting it have power over your confidence, self-belief and the choices you are making about who you are and the life you live.

So, what can you do to silence this horrible voice?

The answer is to take a lesson out of any anti-bullying playbook. To deal with a bully in real life, you need to firmly and clearly say stop, while you hold your head high and walk away. To silence your inner critic, you don't need to debate with it or try to change it – just say 'stop' and then ignore anything else it says.

~~~

Just because your inner critic is speaking,
it doesn't mean you have to listen to what it has to say.

This can seem hard at first. But it's remarkable how quickly the voice in your head will become silent when you stop listening to what it has to say.

When I was first learning how to do this for myself, I would often picture a small child – perhaps it was my inner child – putting its hands over its ears and saying, 'Lalalalala I can't hear you!' as I drove those critical and judgemental thoughts out of my mind. It sounds so funny as an adult to be saying that out loud, but I promise you – it works!

✳ GUARD YOUR ✳
SELF-ESTEEM

Speaking of your inner child, as you develop new ways to boost your confidence and build your self-belief the next thing I want you to do is to make the commitment to never speak to yourself more harshly than you would to a small child.

If you've been in my orbit for a while – read my books or listened to my podcasts – you may have heard me say this before. It's one of the most important lessons I teach and one of the most important rules I follow for myself. We all know that the way to bring out the best in a child is to encourage them, not to berate them.

Think about a child learning to walk, or toilet train – there are lots of tumbles and accidents, but we gloss over them and quickly redirect the child's focus and attention on how well they are doing and how much closer to their target they are getting. We want them to believe in their potential and to know that with each attempt they are getting closer to success.

Why is it then that as adults we so often take the opposite approach with ourselves? Instead of speaking to ourselves in a warm, supportive and encouraging voice, we criticise and berate ourselves and say things like, 'I'm so stupid', 'I'm such an idiot' and often a whole lot worse?

~~~

Encourage yourself by
saying things that lift you up.

When you are interacting with a child, whether it's your child, a relative, family friend, pupil or some other child who crossed your path, in that moment, at the time of your interaction, you are the guardian of that child's self-esteem.

As an adult, you are the guardian of your self-esteem – guard it wisely.

✳ CHEER YOURSELF ON ✳

While we're talking about the way you speak to yourself, the next thing I want you to know is that if you want to build your confidence, not only do you need to give your inner cheerleader a promotion, you also need to fire the drill sergeant inside your head.

Despite what you might see in the movies, people rarely get better at something by being shouted at, intimidated or humiliated. Well, that might not be 100 per cent true … with a humiliating or intimidating approach you could still improve the specific skill you were working on, but the price paid by your confidence and self-belief is rarely going to be worth it.

The role of a cheerleader is to rally the team, remind them of what is possible, call out past victories and help them to keep their head in the game. And this is what I want you to learn to do for yourself.

- ✹ You can do it!
- ✹ I know you have what it takes!
- ✹ You got so close last time!
- ✹ I can't wait to see you succeed!
- ✹ I believe in you!
- ✹ You've got this!

The more you cheer yourself on,
the more your confidence will grow.

When you become your own cheerleader, using positive and encouraging phrases will become automatic and cheering yourself will become the most natural and comfortable thing for you to do.

✳ CHOOSE YOUR ✳ THOUGHTS

Now, while the rallying cry of the words I just shared feels good, there is another reason why saying phrases like this to yourself is so powerful. Your thoughts control your feelings and when you hear these phrases and listen to them – *really listen* – you start to feel better about yourself.

~~~

Choose thoughts that will help you to feel confident –
thoughts that make you feel good about yourself.

You don't have to wait for big events or scary situations to put this into action. You can wake up each morning and say to yourself – 'I believe in you … you've got this' as you brush your teeth, or engage in any of your other morning habits.

For me, it's as I put my moisturiser on in the morning. As you know, I'm not 21 anymore and if I'm not paying attention, I find that when I look in the mirror my inner critic wants to find fault with my reflection. Tired eyes, lines here, grey hairs there, and so on. So, before that mean-spirited voice has the chance to plant any of those thoughts in my head, the first time I look at my reflection each day, I say, 'You've got this … you're doing okay.'

We all have days when we wake up looking or feeling better than others, so on a good day there might be more flourish to my words … but regardless of how I look or how I feel I always start my day with those six words: 'You've got this … you're doing okay.'

And after that, my inner critic doesn't stand a chance.

✳ SAY WHAT YOU ✳ NEED TO HEAR

Now, you already know that you need to ditch your drill sergeant voice, but that doesn't mean that your inner cheerleader's voice needs to be one-size-fits-all. If you are feeling anxious or fearful about something important, a rah-rah approach might be the last thing you need. Instead, you might benefit from gentle words of encouragement that meet you where you are. Your inner cheerleader might want to say something like

✳ 'I know you feel afraid right now …

✳ I'm proud of you just for showing up and having a go.

✳ No matter how this turns out …

✳ I know you're going to be glad that you tried.'

On the other hand, if you're feeling nervous or stressed about something that deep down you know you can do, your cheerleader might want to get you fired up by saying,

✳ 'Go for it!

✳ You can do this!

✳ You know you're better skilled than everyone else.

✳ This job has your name on it.

✳ Go claim it!'

Between the quiet, gentle approach and the high-energy one lie a myriad of other opportunities for your inner cheerleader to give you a boost.

Cheerleading isn't one-size-fits-all –
choose a voice that will make you feel better, not worse.

And if you're not sure what kind of cheerleader you need to be, just ask yourself, 'What would I say to my best friend if they were in my shoes right now?'

Listen to your response and then use it to cheer on the person who needs to hear it: *you.*

✳ ✳ ✳

MARCUS'S CONFIDENCE CRASH COURSE

My dad was super critical of everything I did growing up. It always felt like nothing I did was good enough and, to be honest, even though he passed away five years ago, I still hear his negativity in my head.

I think he genuinely believed he was 'helping me' with his constant criticisms and more than once he told me he was worried that if he said I'd done well, I might stop trying and start to be complacent about success.

Now that I'm a parent I can see that my dad wasn't a bad father ... but he was definitely bad at this part of parenting. I'd *never* speak to my children the way he spoke to me.

But I do speak critically to myself. I'm always saying, 'I'm such an idiot', 'That was really stupid', 'I should have known better', 'What was I thinking?' Step 5: Cheer yourself on made me realise that I actually speak to myself like this *all the time*.

The worst part is, I don't just say these critical comments silently in my head either. And I realise now that when I criticise myself in this way, my children are learning to speak to themselves this way too, and that this is definitely *not* the example I want to set them.

From now on, instead of speaking to my children one way and myself another, I'm going to be encouraging, positive and actively try to build my confidence instead of speaking to myself like my father did and dragging my confidence down.

✳ LOVE YOURSELF ✳

Despite its benefits, the idea of speaking positively and encouragingly to yourself makes a lot of people feel nervous; they worry it will make them big-headed or obnoxious. So the next thing I want you to do is to let go of this baggage from your childhood.

When I was at school, 'She loves herself' was the ultimate insult. We need to reframe this. 'They love themselves' should be the ultimate recognition of someone's self-worth.

Loving yourself is
a sign of self-worth.

I was so proud of my daughter when she was about four and one night at bedtime she was listing all the people who love her. It started with the obvious – parents, grandparents, cousins – and then the circle got wider to include her cousins' grandparents on the other side of their family, her teachers and her nanny … and then she stopped and looked at me with a big smile and said, 'And of course I love me.'

I had to give myself a pat on the back for that one and say, 'Job well done, Mum!' But loving yourself and acknowledging it isn't just for four-year-olds. It is something that we all deserve … at every age.

✳ FOLLOW THE PATH TO ✳ GRACE AND EASE

While we are talking about learning to love yourself, acknowledging that love and speaking to yourself with love and encouragement, I want to explain the true power of the words you use when you speak to yourself – you can speak anything into existence.

Now, I don't mean you can say, 'Abracadabra' and *poof*! whatever you want will appear with no effort on your behalf. But if you speak harshly to yourself, constantly putting yourself down or telling yourself that you are not good enough, you will feel 'not good enough'. Every step you take and effort you make will come from a place of feeling inadequate and unworthy, making your journey to success feel like an uphill battle. But if you continue to speak to yourself with love and encouragement, your confidence and self-belief will grow, which will make everything feel more comfortable and easier for you.

The things you say have a direct impact on the reality you will create.

Whatever life journey you choose, there will still be hills to climb and bumps on the road – but when you develop your confidence and self-belief, you'll find that you can navigate with both grace and ease.

KEY INSIGHTS

STEP 5: CHEER YOURSELF ON

1. Bring out the best in yourself by becoming your own biggest fan.
2. Your inner critic is a bully – ignoring it is the best way to make it go away.
3. Never speak to yourself more harshly than you would to a small child.
4. There is no point in getting better at something at the expense of feeling bad about yourself.
5. The more you cheer yourself on, the more your confidence will grow.
6. Ask yourself, 'What would my best friend say, if they were in my shoes right now?'
7. Loving yourself builds confidence, not obnoxiousness.
8. Believe in yourself – everything feels easier when you feel confident.

JOURNAL PROMPTS

1. Pay attention to the way you have been speaking to yourself: the words you use and the tone you take. Reflect on the impact this has on your confidence and self-belief and make the decision to only speak to yourself in an encouraging way from now on.

2. Think about how you would like to feel at the start of each day. What feelings about yourself do you want to have, and what thoughts will you generate to activate those feelings? Use your answers to create a morning cheer for yourself. Even if you never say it out loud, if you start each day with this new cheer, you can be confident you will be setting yourself up for success.

3. Ask yourself, 'What would be different in my life if I had unconditional belief in myself?' Make a note of the thoughts and feelings that come up for you when you consider this, and then make the decision to live this way from now on.

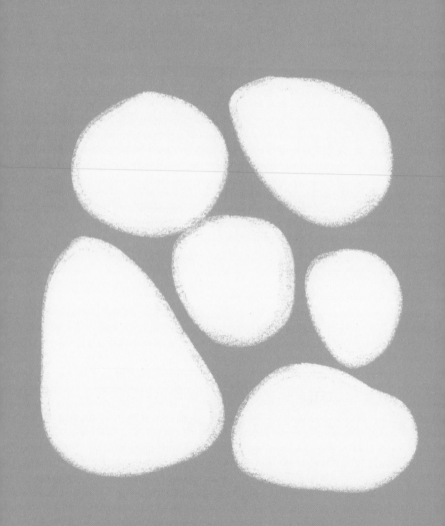

STEP 6:

RISE TO THE CHALLENGE

Everything is easier when you believe in yourself, so learn how to disempower your fears and confidently handle whatever life sends your way.

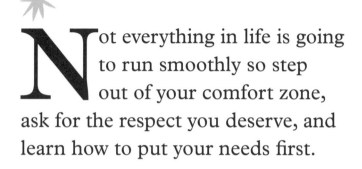

Not everything in life is going to run smoothly so step out of your comfort zone, ask for the respect you deserve, and learn how to put your needs first.

When I finished my rather unsuccessful career as a model, I thought a career in communications would be the perfect next step for me. Unfortunately, nobody else seemed to think the same and I kept getting feedback that I was too old at 24 for a junior position and too inexperienced for the next step. But eventually, a call came that would change my career and my life in ways I had never even imagined.

I was doing a not-amazing-but-at-least-it-pays temp job when I got a call from the recruitment agency asking me a whole lot of technical questions about my skills and whether I would consider myself suitable for a junior accountant role. A junior accountant! I'd done an eight-week bookkeeping course at night school, not a three-year degree in finance! But something about the way the recruiter was asking his questions made me bite my tongue and so instead I said, 'Why do you ask?'

He explained that he was recruiting for a junior in the accounting department of a major international financial institution. Because of the unique nature of this organisation, they had specific geographical staffing quotas that needed to be met. The new recruit for the finance department needed to be Italian. But, the head of the department wanted someone who had English as their first language. The recruiter searched his database for a dual citizen and my name came up – a wild card entry if there ever was one!

I asked the recruiter to send over the job description, took it to the accountant at the company where I was temping, and asked her to explain what all the different tasks and responsibilities meant. I decided that it didn't sound too hard, so I rang the recruiter back and told him I was confident I could do everything on the job description, especially if the organisation were to provide me with some training.

I could almost hear his brain running the numbers on how much money he would make in a placement fee if this wild card entry got the job, versus how hard his boss would kick his butt if I completely embarrassed myself, him and his company in the process. And then, summoning every skerrick of self-belief I could find, I said the line that clinched it for me: 'If you can get me the interview, I can get the job.'

It worked. I did. And the rest is history ... or at least my history.

✳ YOUR MINDSET ✳ MATTERS

The famous quote often attributed to Henry Ford, 'Whether you think you can, or you think you can't – you're right', is right. Your mindset has more bearing on your success or failure than anything else you do. If you want to feel good about who you are and the life you live, you need to believe that this is what you deserve and that you are willing and more than capable of making this the reality of your life.

If you want to feel good about your life,
you need to decide that you are
going to feel good about your life.

While some people might find it easy to feel this way when things are going well, the real skill is in training your mindset so that you can continue to believe in yourself even when things feel tough. So, back to Henry Ford, I want you to decide to believe that you *can* – that the things you want from life are possible for you and that any hurdles or obstacles you meet along the way are things you will be able to handle or overcome with grace and ease.

Making this decision – choosing to think this way – is the first step you need to take to ensure that you feel this way.

✳ OWN YOUR ✳ FEELINGS

But just because you've made the decision to believe in yourself and focus on thoughts that will generate the feelings of confidence and self-belief that you want, it doesn't mean that those new feelings will be instant, or that they will be the only feelings that you have.

You need to own *all* of your feelings: the good, the bad and the downright ugly. This might sound counterintuitive. I can already hear you saying, 'But Domonique, aren't I supposed to be focusing on having positive, optimistic and uplifting thoughts? Why are you telling me I'm supposed to have ugly ones too?' So, I want to make an important distinction here. I want you to *own* your feelings … not to embrace them, roll around in them or wallow in them.

Don't allow your uncomfortable and unpleasant feelings to consume you or push your other feelings out of the way.

When you take ownership of your feelings, you acknowledge and accept them and give yourself permission to be curious about them. Instead of sweeping your unpleasant feelings under the carpet, bottling them up or engaging in behaviours that numb them – comfort eating, over-drinking or shopping to name just a few – when you take ownership of your not-so-pleasant feelings and examine them with curiosity and without judgement, you are able to see the lessons they hold. Those less-than-attractive and even downright ugly feelings will give you an insight into the thoughts you have and the thoughts you might not have realised you have – the limiting beliefs you hold and fears you may have been buying into.

Once you've taken ownership of your feelings, examined them in a judgement-free way and extracted the lessons they hold, you will know *exactly* what new thoughts you need to focus on creating in order to release these unpleasant feelings and generate authentically empowering ones instead.

✳ FACE YOUR FEARS ✳

Now that you know that you need to own your feelings rather than numb them, squash them down or bottle them up I want to prepare you for one of the most uncomfortable feelings of them all: fear. Even though I'm talking about emotional fears, not things that go bump in the night, these fears can still run the gamut from slowly creeping up on you to shocking you and leaving you gasping for air.

Although these fears are different to your instinctive or intuitive fears – the kind that tell you you're in genuine physical danger – your emotional fears are still a message from your subconscious about impending danger. It's just that this time the danger your fears are warning you about is an emotional danger. But as unpleasant as embarrassment, rejection, humiliation, or any of the emotional dangers your fear is trying to protect you from are, they're rarely likely to be fatal!

*Your fears are your limiting
beliefs brought to life.*

When you find yourself experiencing fear – whether it's fear of failure, fear of success, fear of judgement or any other kind of fear – I want you to take the same approach as you have with your other unpleasant feelings. Begin by acknowledging your fear. Notice where you feel it in your body – you'll usually feel it in the pit of your stomach, rising to your solar plexus, and it may get as high as a tight feeling in your chest.

Rather than give in to this feeling or run away from it, hide from it or numb it, I want you to breathe *through* it. Just because a feeling is unpleasant, it doesn't mean that you won't survive it. Remind yourself that your fears are your subconscious protecting you from emotional risk. It is protecting your heart and soul, but your life itself is perfectly safe and secure.

When you find yourself experiencing fear, whether you knew you would feel afraid or it took you completely by surprise, instead of running from it or doing something to avoid it, challenge yourself to be present to it while you move through it.

✳ CHALLENGE YOURSELF ✳

So now that you know the best way to disempower your fear is to challenge yourself to keep moving forward in spite of it, the next thing I want you to know is that if you want to build your self-belief, you need to keep on challenging yourself. Not just with the thing that triggered your fear, but by challenging yourself in life, in general.

You can challenge yourself to try new things, make new friends, or go on new adventures. You can try a new sport, experiment with a new hobby or learn a new skill.

Your comfort zone is where
your self-confidence goes to die.

Life in your comfort zone might feel easy, but your self-belief is like a muscle: it needs to be exercised regularly to keep it strong. And, it's not the outcome that matters. It's not that each thing that you try needs to be a roaring success; if you're anything like most people, when you step outside of your comfort zone you'll crash and burn at least some of the time.

But, regardless of the outcome, your confidence and self-belief will thank you for it. When you try something new or challenge yourself in some way the message your subconscious hears is that you're worth it. You were worth the risk, worth the investment of time, money or energy. You didn't need a guaranteed outcome to take the chance. You deserved to try.

✳ STAND UP FOR ✳ YOURSELF

One of the great benefits of hearing that message loud and clear – that you're worth it – is that it makes it easier to stand up for yourself and to stop accepting less than what you are worth in other parts of your life. When I talk about recognising your worth and standing up for yourself, I'm not just talking about finally finding the courage to ask for a pay rise – although if that's something you've been thinking about, you should go for it. What I'm talking about here is much broader than any measure of financial value.

I don't want you to just think about what your time is worth, I want you to remember that you are a worthwhile human being and you deserve to be treated that way. You might need to ask your colleague to stop interrupting you, tell your teenagers that you are not their personal Uber driver or that you're not running a hotel. Or you might need to remind your partner that sometimes you want to choose what show you watch on TV.

Learn how to say, 'I matter.
My thoughts feelings and opinions matter.
My time matters and so does my energy.'

Now you may feel a surge of energy just at hearing those words – or you may feel that it triggers yet another fear. And standing up for yourself can be challenging and uncomfortable. It might lead to an argument or heated discussion. The person you are speaking to might huff and puff or give you the cold shoulder treatment.

Remind yourself that all you are asking for is to be treated with the respect that you deserve and that, while these experiences might be uncomfortable, they are survivable.

✳ APPLY THE ✳ FORMULA

If you do need to have a challenging conversation my favourite approach is to apply this formula:

When you … ➙ I feel … ➙ and what I need is …

Step one is to describe the other person's actions in a factual and emotionally neutral way. Step two is to describe your feelings without blame or accusation. And step three is to calmly but assertively state what you need.

For example, I recently used this approach with my teenager. I said to her, 'When I collect you from school, and you and your friend get in the car without acknowledging me (I described the behaviour) I feel like an invisible service provider (I described my feelings without blame). And what I need is for you to say "Hi Mum, how are you?" and then I'm more than happy for you and your friend to go back to the conversation you were having (I stated my needs).'

When you … ➙ I feel … ➙ and what I need is …

The beauty of this approach is that you are not blaming the other person. You are letting them know how you feel and taking responsibility for your needs. When I used this approach with my daughter, she said straight away, 'I'm sorry Mum, I didn't even realise I did that. Thanks for coming to get me from school.' No arguments, explosive emotions or meltdowns.

Stand up for yourself,
express your dissatisfaction,
calmly and with a cool head and
explain what needs to change and how.

You could follow the same approach with that colleague who keeps interrupting you, or you could be more direct: 'I am in the middle of a sentence, please don't interrupt me.'

This is a perfectly reasonable thing to say, and while they might not like hearing it – and your knees might shake while you say it – your confidence and self-belief will soar because you did it.

MIRANDA'S CONFIDENCE CRASH COURSE

When I had my children, I thought I could never love anyone more – and then my grandchildren came along. There aren't even words to tell you how much I adore those kids ... but although my love knows no bounds, my patience definitely has its limits, and lately it's been seriously tested.

Three years ago I decided to reduce my working hours and begin my semi-retirement. I wanted to work less so I could be around my grandchildren more ... but I never said anything about becoming their nanny, tutor or full-time babysitter, or that spending time with my grandchildren was the only thing I wanted to do.

It felt like as soon as I cut back my working hours as a pharmacist my children thought they had my help with their children on demand.

I didn't even notice it at first – I was happy to help and be a part of their lives. But what started out as a 'I'm sorry it's such late notice but is there any chance you could mind the children' has turned into me feeling like I'm an on-call service provider – my children assume I have no other plans, that I'm always available to mind their children at short notice and for all the hours that they want me to.

This is not what this was supposed to be like.

I've been feeling angry and resentful, but I didn't know how to address the issue without it sounding like I don't enjoy my grandchildren. It got so bad that I started thinking about going back to work full time, just so I could stop them from taking me for granted.

But thanks to Step 6: Rise to the challenge, I have a better plan. Although I'm a little nervous, now that I have the 'When you ... → I feel ... → and what I need is ...' plan, I feel confident I can make them understand.

They might not like it at first, but it's time for me to say it and for them to hear it.

✳ YOUR NEEDS ✳
MATTER

Now that you have learned a few tips for standing up for yourself and asking for what you need, I want you to shift your needs from the bottom of your list and move them a whole lot closer to the top. The important people in your life won't suffer greatly if they come second for a change and, while you won't always be able to put your needs first, I want you to make sure they are at least in the top three.

Putting yourself first doesn't mean
you have to put everyone else last.

When I think about the most important needs in my life, I think about the needs of my family, the needs of my partnership and my needs. The important thing about my list is that this is not a hierarchy where I come third. It's more of a trinity or balancing act, where my family, my partnership and I have to take turns at making sure we all get what we need. If everything becomes about the family, I feel resentful – but if I only ever do what I want, I might feel neglectful.

Life is a balancing act, but, even if you've got a lot of balls in the air, I want to make sure your needs are at least one of the balls you are juggling.

✳ ACT WITH INTEGRITY ✳

So now you've added 'juggler' to the list of new challenges you're going to take on, one thing I want you to know you never have to juggle is your sense of right and wrong. If you want to feel good about who you are and the life you live, you need to do the right thing, not the easy thing. Your integrity, your instinctive understanding of what is right, is something you should never compromise, even when it feels like the hardest thing in the world.

Sometimes the challenge may be to distance yourself from a situation or relationship you are uncomfortable with, other times it might mean speaking up or asking someone to stop if they are doing something that you know is wrong.

Believe in yourself,
act with integrity and know that,
even when doing the right thing can feel hard at the time,
doing the wrong things will feel much worse.

If you find yourself in a situation that challenges your integrity, I want you to know that this is one of the most important challenges you can ever face, and also one of the hardest. But, as hard as it might be, when you face this challenge with courage and integrity, the way you will feel about yourself will be something no one can ever take away.

KEY
INSIGHTS

STEP 6: RISE TO THE CHALLENGE

1. Mindset is everything – decide to feel good about yourself and your life.
2. Own all of your feelings, just don't wallow in them.
3. Your fears are your limiting beliefs brought to life.
4. Your comfort zone is where your self-confidence goes to die – rescue it!
5. Your thoughts, feelings and opinions matter.
6. Your confidence will soar every time you stand up for yourself.
7. Putting yourself first doesn't mean you have to put everyone else last.
8. Confidence and integrity go hand in hand, so do the right thing, not the easy thing.

JOURNAL PROMPTS

1. Reflect on how you normally manage your uncomfortable feelings – do you bottle them up, push them away or engage in things that numb them so you can ignore them? Ask yourself, 'What would be different if I owned and accepted all of my feelings?'

2. Make a note of four simple ways you can step out of your comfort zone. Make the commitment to take one of these actions each week for the next month. At the end of the month, reflect on how stepping outside of your comfort zone has affected the way you feel about yourself and your life.

3. Think of an area of your life where you know you need to stand up for yourself. Consider the *When you …* → *I feel …* → *and what I need is …* formula and write out your declaration. Notice how just writing it down has an impact on your confidence and self-belief – and then make the commitment to put it into action.

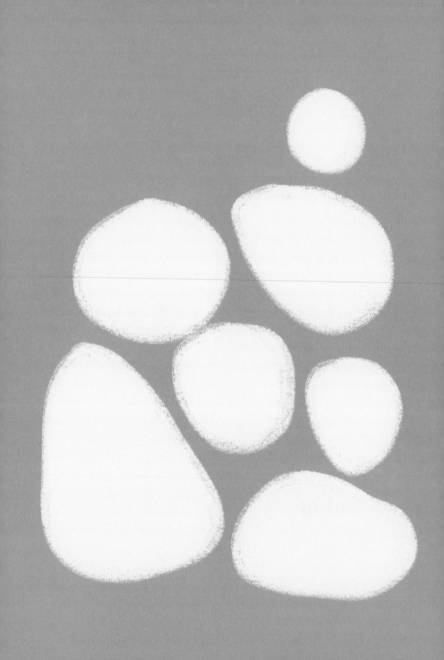

STEP 7:

SHINE YOUR LIGHT

Work out what you really want
and embrace a brighter future
for your life.

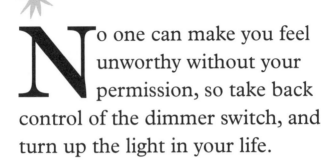

No one can make you feel unworthy without your permission, so take back control of the dimmer switch, and turn up the light in your life.

I'll never forget my first day at school the year I turned 10.

Unfortunately, I remember it for all the wrong reasons. That day was the first day of what was to be a horrible period in my life: a time in my life when I was bullied daily. It went on for a long time – most of that year – but eventually my bully moved on.

For the next 30 years, I did my best not to think about that time in my life, but something happened in my early forties that brought it back to the front of my mind. I was approached by a magazine for an article they were doing about bullying. The article involved asking people who had been bullied as children to write a letter to their bully from the wisdom of adulthood. Did I know anyone who had been bullied who might want to write about it?

'Eh … me? I could write about my experience.' To this day I don't know what made me say that, why I chose that time in my life to unearth the hurt and humiliation that had been buried for over 30 years. I cried as I wrote my piece. I cried in a way I hadn't let myself cry at the time for fear of showing my weakness. But writing the article was a turning point for me.

I realised that the impact of being bullied hadn't just been limited to my 10-year-old self. It turns out it wasn't something that I had 'gotten over'; it had a very real and profound effect on my life. After I wrote that article, I began to notice all the different ways I had been hiding my light over the years. It wasn't obvious to anyone else – I write books, I work for big corporations, I speak on stages where I literally stand in the spotlight, and I have no trouble standing up for myself or standing up to bullies at this point in my life. But I could still see that there were plenty of small, subtle examples of how I had hidden my light, avoided being seen and protected myself.

I realised as I set about softening and healing this scar that I was the one in charge of my light now – and, while things had happened that made me want to dim my light in the past, I was in charge of how brightly it shone in my future.

✳ SHINE BRIGHTLY ✳

The first thing I want you to do as you decide to stop hiding your light is to realise that nobody else is in control of that dimmer switch except for you. While it might feel like the people around you, experiences from your past, or your personal circumstances have had a role to play, nothing can keep you in the dark or stop you from shining as brightly as you deserve – unless you let it.

I want to be clear here. I'm not trying to diminish the influence these factors can have. I'm not saying there aren't reasons why you've felt like you've needed to hide your light, or be less in some way than all you have the potential to be. What I am saying is that the *reasons* why things have been this way in the past, don't need to become your *excuses* for things staying this way in the future.

*Take full responsibility for how
you feel about yourself, your life,
and what you do or don't do with it
from this point forward.*

If in the past you received unwanted negative attention of any kind, just for being you, it makes sense that you might want to keep a little bit of yourself hidden.

Perhaps you too were bullied. Maybe you were always being told to be quiet, that you were being too much. Maybe you received unwanted sexual attention or advances or were subjected to inappropriate or hostile criticism.

If the reasons why you have held yourself back and learned to hide your light are far more serious or traumatic than the examples I have given here, I want you to know that your past still doesn't need to define your future. It might be hard work and the journey might take you a little longer, but as a survivor you still get to choose a future where you can thrive.

I hope that you'll find it easy to take responsibility for your personal dimmer switch now that you know you have one. You might be like me, and find it easy in most areas of your life – but there may still be some experiences that trigger you. You will need to work harder at those times to make sure that you don't dim your light. I know I still worry about the first day back at school, even when it's one of my children's first days and not mine!

But if you find that trying to reclaim your light re-traumatises you, you might find that you need the support of a psychologist, therapist or counsellor to embrace a brighter future for yourself.

✳ BE THE HERO ✳ OF YOUR LIFE

While I'm sifting through the memories of my school days, I can remember that one of the most popular hit songs of my teenage years was 'Holding Out for a Hero' by Bonnie Tyler, from the film *Footloose*. But what works as a hit in an '80s film isn't necessarily good advice for life.

I keep hearing people tell me that they're waiting for someone or something, to make everything in their life okay. And I'm not just talking about people who are holding out for Mr or Miss Right, those who never heard that 'a man is not a financial plan' or thought a woman would come along and take care of them just like their mother did.

I hear people speak as if their job will be their hero: 'If only I could get a promotion everything would be okay in my life.' Or even their house – they tell me that they'll start living their life when they've bought the right house, or a new sofa for the house, or paid off the house, or renovated the house. I think you get where I'm heading.

Instead of waiting for a hero to come along – whether it's another person or a different situation or circumstance – I want you to decide *to be the hero* of your life. Imagine what would be different if you took full responsibility for your future – if, regardless of what has or hasn't happened to you right up until this point, you decided that from now on, you were the one responsible for your life and that you were going to make sure it was one you want to be living?

~~~

It's up to you, and you alone,
to take responsibility for your life.

✳ DITCH YOUR ✳ EXCUSES

It's time to get up close and personal with some of the other excuses you've been using: the stories you've been telling yourself to explain why you're not doing the things that are within your power – things that you know you need to do – to feel good about who you are and the life you live. Whether it's exercising regularly and eating well, sticking to your budget and paying down your credit card or simply stopping the scroll and getting the sleep you need, when you don't make an effort to do the things you know you need to do in order to feel good, it sends a message to your subconscious that you're not worth the effort.

Which it quickly abbreviates to 'you're not worth it'.

The same thing happens when you don't keep your commitments to yourself (or others) or when you say you're going to take action or make progress on a goal or intention, and instead you just let it drift.

*When you accept less than what
you know you want and deserve from life,
your subconscious accepts this
as proof that you're not worth it.*

From now on, every time you need to do something that you know will make you feel good about yourself – regardless of how much effort it requires in the moment – I want you to flick your hair (literally or metaphorically), pretend you are in an advertisement for L'Oréal and say, 'It's *because I'm worth it.*'

✳ DECIDE WHO YOU ✳ WANT TO BE

For all this talk about committing to doing the things you need to do to feel good about who you are and the life you live, I want to make sure you don't fall into the trap of focusing your efforts and attention on the wrong things. I want you to cast your mind back to Step 1 and remember that this has nothing to do with trying to be perfect.

And this is not about attempting to be the person you think you *should* be to uphold some social norm or stereotype, or to compete with the images you see in your feed.

As you think about what it is that you *do* need to focus your attention and efforts on, I want you to remember that this is about being the person *you want to be*. I know you might immediately say, 'But I don't know what I want to do', so let me share one of my favourite quotes from the iconic fashion designer Diane von Fürstenberg.

In her memoir, *The Woman I Wanted to Be*, Diane said, 'I didn't know what I wanted to do, but I always knew the woman I wanted to be.'

So, let me ask you:

Who do you want to be?

How do you want to show up in the world?

What do you want to be known for? Remembered for?

These are important questions, ones that so many people have never taken a moment to consider let alone formulate their answers to. But while these are big questions, they don't need to have big answers. You don't need to say, 'I want to be an astrophysicist', 'I want to cure cancer', or 'I want to be remembered for changing the world.'

Your answers can be much simpler but that doesn't make them any less important. You might say, 'I want to be a good person, who makes people feel welcome wherever they go, and who is known for always having an open heart and mind.' Or something like, 'I want to be successful doing work I love, while still having the time and energy to enjoy my family.'

Simply showing up in life and saying,
'I want to be the best version of me I can be'
is enough to set your confidence and
self-belief on the right track.

PAULA'S CONFIDENCE
CRASH COURSE

When I was a child, whenever anyone asked me what I wanted to do when I grew up, I always said 'be a mummy'. I've always wanted children … but not just children, I wanted the whole picture: a husband, a nice house and all that goes with it.

And that's exactly what I have.

And I'm definitely not complaining. My husband might not be perfect, but he is a good man who takes care of our family and loves his children. We live in a lovely house in a good area, the children go to great schools and my life looks as close to my childhood vision as possible.

But deep down, I've known for a while something was missing. I've dedicated my life to my children and my family. And for the longest time, I've been happy to do it. But now that they're older, they don't need me the way they once did and sometimes I feel like I'm just their driver …

Being a mother is still the most important thing I do, but it just doesn't feel as meaningful and purposeful as it once did. I realise it's time for me to take responsibility for *my* life. I've got a lot of good years yet. I don't want to feel sad about my upcoming empty nest, I want to feel excited about being able to fly the coop too!

I realise that for the longest time I've been living my life through everyone else. Being a good wife and homemaker for my husband, being a good mother to my children. I love those things, but I think I've also let these roles define me. And it's time for me to start thinking about how I want to define myself.

After reading Step 7: Shine your light I've been asking myself some big questions: 'What do I want from the rest of my life?' and 'What am I willing to do, or not do, to have it?'

I don't have all my answers yet but I'm doing my best to be, as Domonique says, comfortable with the discomfort and trust that my answers will come.

✳ FIND YOUR ✳
INNER COMPASS

So often people can hear an inner whisper of what they really want for themselves and from their lives – but rather than listen to these whispers and see what insights they hold, they push them back down and do their best to ignore them in the hope that they will go away.

Except, of course, they don't.

Those whispers – those quiet, internal knowings – come from your inner compass, the part inside of you that knows where your true north is, even when you can't see it or haven't intentionally set it. The main reason most people can't hear their answer is because they've become so skilled at not listening for it.

While you're asking yourself these big bold questions,
I want you to really listen to your answers.

But if, when you ask yourself these questions, you don't have any inkling of your answer, I want you to know that's okay too. You just don't know your answer *yet*. Just relax in the silence, knowing that if you open your heart and mind to these questions, in time your answers will come.

✻ BREATHE THROUGH IT ✻

For some people, it can be confronting to discover that their inner compass has just as much power to guide them forward as their inner critic has to hold them back. If you've spent your adult life being led by expectations and held back by your fears, believing your limiting beliefs and buying into those of everyone else as well, seeing your potential open up like this can be breathtaking.

Or it can feel like a sucker punch that takes your breath away.

If this happens to you, please don't run away from this feeling, or treat this voice like a genie and attempt to shove it back in the bottle. As I said in the first few pages of this book, if you want to feel good about who you are and the life you live, you need to get comfortable with discomfort instead of numbing yourself, ignoring it, or doing whatever you can to run away from it.

Get comfortable with discomfort –
it's a sign of good things to come.

As you sit with the realisation that this is your life, and you get to decide how to live it, I want you to know that, as uncomfortable as this feeling can be … this is a good thing. Imagine a butterfly trying to break out of its cocoon. I'm not a biologist, but I reckon it's messy and uncomfortable but feels oh so worth it once it gets the chance to spread its wings.

✸ TAKE YOUR TIME ✸

This is not an invitation to pressure yourself or to feel like you have to overhaul anything you are unhappy about overnight. The good news is, unlike a butterfly, which lives for about a month if it is lucky, you have *plenty* of time to make the changes you want or need to make in your life. Rome wasn't built in a day and you want to make sure you don't throw the baby out with the bathwater. As old as these sayings might be, they're exactly what you need to hear right now.

Instead of rushing to take action,
commit to taking responsibility and to making
any changes you need to make, responsibly.

 FOCUS ON YOUR FUTURE

Even though I've told you not to panic and try to change every-thing all at once, I want you to know that this is an invitation to be patient, not complacent. Regardless of the past, now is the time to shift your focus to the future. Who do you want to be and what life do you want to create for yourself?

The responsibility to be the person
you want to be and live the life
you want to live is yours and yours alone.

Take time to consider your answers. And then, when you're ready, shine your light on them and make them your reality.

KEY INSIGHTS

STEP 7: SHINE YOUR LIGHT

1. Your past doesn't need to define your future.
2. Don't wait for anyone or anything to save you – decide to be the hero of your life.
3. If you don't make an effort your subconscious will believe you weren't worth it.
4. Decide what kind of person you want to be.
5. Learn to listen to your inner compass – it knows the right answer, even if you don't.
6. Get comfortable with discomfort, it's a sign of good things to come.
7. Take responsibility and make any changes you need to make, responsibly.
8. Focus on what you want from the future and make it your reality.

✳
JOURNAL
PROMPTS

1. Examine your self-talk and ask yourself, 'What am I waiting for?' See if you can identify the obstacles, real and imagined, that you have placed in your path. Once you've made your list, for each item, ask yourself, 'Do I really need to let this stop me?' Once you have your answers commit to taking action that moves you forward wherever and whenever you can.

2. Think about who you want to be and write a detailed description of that person – you might find it easier to write this in the third person, as if you are talking about someone else and not yourself. Once you know who you want to be, choose one small action that will help you to get closer to who you want to become.

3. One of the best ways to access your inner compass and find out where your personal true north lies is through meditation or guided visualisation. Sit or lie somewhere comfortable with your eyes closed and ask yourself the question, 'What do I really want from … ?' Each time you ask the question, notice the thoughts that come up for you and how they make you feel. Keep track of these thoughts and feelings in your journal. Over time your thoughts will come into sharper focus and your true north will become clear.

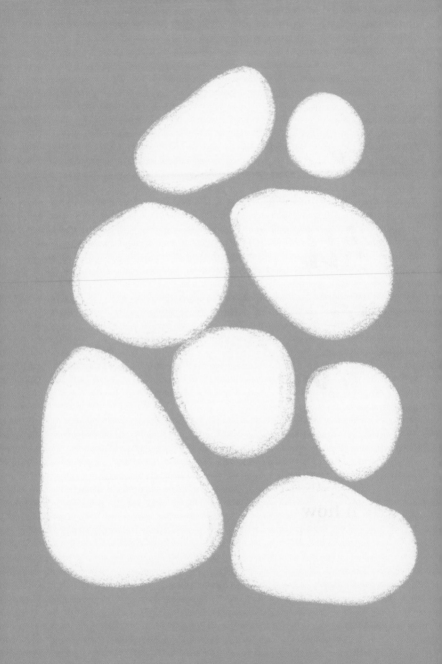

STEP 8:

FALL IN LOVE WITH YOURSELF

See yourself through the eyes of someone who loves you and learn how to show yourself the same love.

The most important relationship you will ever have is with yourself, so respect your boundaries, forgive your failings and become the star in the love story of your life.

As you've probably noticed by now, I like to start each chapter with a little anecdote or story from my own life. I like to share how I learned the key lessons of each chapter and how I've been applying them to my life. But as I sat down to prepare for this chapter my mind drew a blank ... what story could I tell you that would encourage you to fall in love with yourself?

After racking my brain for a couple of days it finally hit me and I knew why nothing was presenting itself – because it wasn't my story to tell.

This chapter is all about *your* story. The story you get to write for yourself, about who you are and the life you live.

And it's my hope that the story you write will be a great love story. Not because it is filled with romance with some other wonderful person (although that might be nice too) but because you finally realise that the special person leading the story is you.

✶ BUILD A GOOD ✶ RELATIONSHIP

The first thing I want you to do as you begin to write this love story is to recognise that the relationship you have with yourself is the most important relationship of your life. Not because I've taken out shares in Hallmark greeting cards, inspirational fridge magnets or car bumper stickers, but because the way you feel about yourself will underpin every other relationship in your life.

*The quality of your relationship
with yourself will determine the quality
of all your other relationships.*

Want a good marriage? Have a good relationship with yourself. A great relationship with your children, close friend-ships, supportive co-workers? A healthy relationship with your parents? The experience you have in each of these relationships, and every other relationship in your life, will be determined by the quality of the relationship you have with yourself.

I'm not saying that each of these relationships will be perfect or that you are in control of how a particular relationship turns out – sometimes you will need to put firm boundaries in place, distance yourself or walk away from a relationship altogether.

But your ability to do this – to prioritise protecting yourself and your self-esteem – will be a direct result of your confidence, self-belief and the investment you've made in creating a loving and respectful relationship with yourself.

✸ SEE YOUR BEAUTY ✸

They say beauty is in the eye of the beholder. So, with that in mind, the next thing I want you to focus on as you fall in love with yourself is just how beautiful you are. I don't mean you need to look in the mirror and see Gal Gadot or Chris Hemsworth looking back at you – though lucky you, if you do!

See your beauty on the inside while learning
not to criticise whatever you see on the outside.

Throughout this book, I've talked about paying attention to your positive qualities and ignoring your inner critic but now it's time to step things up a level.

It's time to see yourself through the eyes of someone who loves you and cares about you deeply. It doesn't matter if the person whose perspective you adopt is your partner, your child, a parent, a friend, or a grandparent. Just focus on someone you know who has you on their 'my favourite people' list, and think about how they would describe you.

They might describe your smile, your willingness to help a friend or the way you make everyone feel welcome. Or perhaps they'd talk about how smart you are, the sound of your laugh or the way your eyes sparkle when you smile. Or maybe they'd talk about your kindness, patience and the way that spending time with you feels like being enveloped in a hug – even when you're not together in person.

If you really want to give your confidence a boost you could even try writing this in the third person. Imagine this person – this someone who loves you – was writing about you. For example, if I chose my best friend, I might write, 'Domonique is always smiling … even if she is crying. I can say anything I want to her and I know she will never judge me. She makes everyone feel welcome, she cooks delicious food and loves to make simple things look beautiful.'

Well, she sounds nice – I'd like to be friends with her!

As you think (or write) about yourself from your loved one's perspective, you don't have to believe them or agree with them – just learn to see yourself as if you *were* them.

❊ MAKE GRATITUDE ❊
YOUR ATTITUDE

Now that you've started to see a little more of the beauty in yourself, I want you to widen your perspective and start to see more of the beauty in your life and acknowledge the things you have to be grateful for. No matter where your life is at right now – even if you feel that some things are missing or aren't working as well as you want them to – I have no doubt that you still have many things to be grateful for. Even if they're not at the top of your mind.

Some people think of gratitude as something you do occasionally when you remember it or something particularly good happens. Others speak of it as a daily practice – a series of thoughts that you engage in or a journal that you write in at a specific time each day.

Although I do have a daily gratitude practice – I make a note of what I am grateful for on my brilliant day planner (I've included a copy for you in the workbook that goes with this book) – my real aim is to make gratitude my way of *being*.

Instead of turning your focus
to gratitude at specific times,
feel grateful – all of the time.

When I wake up, I acknowledge that it is good to be alive; when I open the fridge I'm grateful that there is food in it. If the fridge looks a bit empty, I'm grateful I can afford to buy food to put in it. And on and on throughout the day I go.

It doesn't take up any time or energy – these quick thoughts just pop up throughout my day. Pick up my son after school, and I'm grateful for his health and his smile. Help my daughter with her homework and I'm grateful that I am able to help. Even when something annoys me or frustrates me, after I acknowledge my feelings I switch on my gratitude filter to help me to let my frustrations go.

Just the other day I had a long-winded, multi-phone-call issue I had to resolve with my bank. It was excruciating and it did feel like a waste of time – time that I would never get back. When the issue was finally resolved, I politely expressed my frustrations to the bank representative who was helping me. She sympathised but explained (as I fully expected) that there was nothing that she could do. I put down the phone and exhaled deeply. I let go of all the tension that had been building and reminded myself to be grateful that I had the money that the whole conversation with the bank had been about.

Making gratitude your attitude in this way might seem awkward at first, but, like any habit, if you keep it up it will soon come naturally and easily to you. And you will feel much better about your life because of it!

✹ UNCOVER ✹ YOUR VALUES

Now that you're feeling more gratitude for life as it is, I want you to start thinking about life as it could be … life as you *want it* to be. We've already talked about focusing less on your goals and more on your intentions: your personal true north. It's time now to go even deeper and start thinking about your values.

If you want the love you have for yourself to be a lasting one, you need to take the time to get to know yourself on a deeper level. Your values are like the DNA of your soul. They are unique to you and part of what makes you, you – and unless you take time to understand them, you will always be misunderstanding yourself.

Whenever I am asked what the secret is to a happy and fulfilling life, I always answer that the first and most important thing is to live your life in alignment with your values. This means working out what matters most to you and then getting as much of that as possible in your life.

*Your values are the things
that matter most to you in life.*

Most people never stop to think about their values. I even had one client tell me that she could recite her company values off by heart but had no idea about her own. She told me she didn't even know she was supposed to have values and that she thought that thinking about values was just something that marketing departments got big companies to do. How wrong she was.

If you want to feel good about who you are and the life you live, taking the time to discover your values and then making the commitment to living in alignment with them is one of the most important things you can do.

✳ GET TO THE HEART ✳ OF THE MATTER

When most people start thinking about their values, they usually begin with the generic: my health, my family, security and so on. But the key when you are defining your values is to get specific about what really matters to you, and so the next thing I want you to do is to 'peel your onion'.

Imagine your values are like an onion: as you peel each layer you discover another one underneath until you get to the heart of what matters most to you. Take for example health – I've never met someone who doesn't value their health. But everyone values different things about their health.

My values for health are vitality and energy – that means that what matters most to me about my health is that I feel vital and energised and make decisions that help me to maintain that as a natural state in my life. But I know that for one of my super athletic friends, their values for health are around fitness and stamina. This friend enjoys what to me are superhuman feats of endurance and exercises with a ferocity that seems unfathomable to me.

Which is exactly the point. It doesn't matter how that level of exercise feels to me – what matters is that my friend is honouring their values and that I honour mine. While we both value our health, the best way for me to maintain my vitality and energy might be to rest while the most effective way for them to honour their values of fitness and stamina might be to push through and go one more round.

Everyone's values are different.
Find your unique way of expressing yours.

BRYAN'S CONFIDENCE CRASH COURSE

I think for the longest time, I've been waiting to feel confident. I thought it would come when I'd achieved certain things, like when I got married or got a promotion or achieved a certain time in an event I'd been training for.

But I can see now that all of these things exist outside of me. And sure, they give me a boost at the time, like my last triathlon was a PB, but the boost I feel wears off real quick.

I've realised that although I don't feel 'bad' about myself, I'm not actively making sure I feel good about myself either. Sometimes I feel good about myself and sometimes I feel pretty ordinary, but I haven't been the one in control of that feeling.

Step 8: Fall in love with yourself made me stop and realise that I can do something about how I want to feel. Like, I train my body to be strong and withstand challenges – I can train my mindset too, so my self-belief is more resilient to the ups and downs of life.

From now on, I'm also going to be a lot more mindful of the things that matter most to me and make sure I get enough of them in my life. I always make time for my training, but the truth is, it's not the only important thing in my life – I often neglect my other values and then feel guilty about it, like when I feel too busy to call my parents and then feel bad about myself for being too busy to call. That's definitely not helpful to my self-belief.

I really heard Domonique when she said explained how important it is to have a good relationship with yourself – from now on that's something I'm really going to prioritise.

✳ PROTECT YOUR ✳ BOUNDARIES

Every healthy relationship needs clear boundaries to help it to thrive. The one you have with yourself is no different, so once you know what your values are you will want to put clear boundaries in place to respect them.

If your values are the things that matter most to you in life, it makes sense that you should prioritise and protect them. But for most people, this isn't the case at all. They find themselves putting everyone else's wants, needs and priorities well ahead of their own.

When you know what your values are not only does it make it much easier to put the boundaries you need in place, it also gives you a clear understanding of why those boundaries need to be there and how to express the decisions you are making to protect them.

If you find yourself needing to create boundaries or defend them, the simplest language you can use is to say, 'It's important to me ... '. When you tell someone that something is important to you, it is very hard for them to argue with you or to try to convince you that what is important to them is more important than the things that are important to you.

STEP 8: FALL IN LOVE WITH YOURSELF

*When you declare that
something is important to you,
it's hard for anyone to argue with you
or to try to convince you otherwise.*

Let's look at some examples:

* I need to leave work at 5 pm to collect my child from day care. It's important to me that I am there on time.
* No thank you, I don't want a piece of cake. It's important to me that I maintain my diet.
* I won't be joining you at the theatre, I'm on a budget this month and it's important to me that I stick to it.
* No, I don't want to stay up and watch another episode – it's important to me that I get enough sleep.

'It's important to me.'

What a powerful statement that is – one that, when backed up by a clear understanding of your values, becomes impossible to try to argue with.

✻ FORGIVE YOURSELF ✻

If understanding your boundaries is about respecting yourself, the next thing you need to do to boost your confidence and build your self-belief is to learn to forgive yourself – for the things you've done, and, just as importantly, for the things you've failed to do.

We all mess up … each and every one of us. If you're like most people, you can probably give me a list of your mistakes, mishaps and missteps off the top of your head. But while there is value in the lessons learned from these events there is nothing to be gained from beating yourself up about them. Likewise, if you've set out to do something and failed or said you were going to do something and never even got started, you need to forgive yourself for that too.

I'd love to tell you that from here on in, your life will be nothing but smooth sailing, but the truth is, I'm almost certain you're going to encounter some rain or even storms along the way. The worst of these times will be when you feel like you have no one but yourself to blame. When this happens, I want you to remember the lessons of Step 1 and remember that you are not expected to be perfect. Instead of being harsh on yourself, I want you to be *kind* to yourself.

When you love someone, you are kind to them and supportive of them. And when they fall down, you're there to help them to get back up again – not to do what you can to keep them down. It's time to direct that compassionate approach towards yourself.

〰

Learn your lesson,
forgive yourself for the past and
move forward confidently to your future.

This isn't about giving yourself a 'get out of jail' card or a free ride through life, but there is a big difference between holding yourself accountable and holding yourself hostage. Holding on to bitterness and resentment, even if it is towards yourself, will eat away at your confidence. And allowing feelings of guilt and shame to grow or linger is guaranteed to erode your self-belief.

✳ CLAIM YOUR ✳ FUTURE

As you head forward to towards your future, I want to finish this chapter in the same place that we began – by focusing on your story.

What do you want to be able to say
about who you are and the life you live?

I want you to imagine what your life would be like if you moved forward with complete confidence – to imagine what it would feel like if you experienced nothing but total self-belief. And then, instead of waiting for that magical day to happen, I want you to go and claim that future of yours, knowing that the best way to build your confidence and self-belief is by taking action.

KEY
INSIGHTS

STEP 8: FALL IN LOVE WITH YOURSELF

1. Your relationship with yourself is the most important relationship you will ever have.
2. See yourself through the eyes of someone who loves you.
3. Make gratitude your attitude – pay attention to all the things you are grateful for.
4. Live your life in alignment with your values; they are the DNA of your soul.
5. Take the time to get to the heart of what matters most to you.
6. Protect your boundaries by declaring, 'It's important to me ... '
7. Forgive yourself for the things you've done and the things you've failed to do.
8. Claim your future – the best way to build your confidence is by taking action.

JOURNAL PROMPTS

1. Think about the healthiest, most positive relationship in your life. What qualities does this relationship have that make it so rewarding? What would be different in your life if your relationship with yourself had the same qualities?

2. When do you find it hardest to set or maintain boundaries in your life? Make a list of all the times you find it hard to say 'no'. Write out your 'It's important to me ... ' statement for each one, so that you're ready to firmly state your boundaries next time you need to.

3. Describe yourself in the third person the way someone presenting an award to you might introduce you to an audience* ... but set this description at some imaginary point in your future. Include your strengths, positive qualities, as well as your existing and future achievements and successes. To make it feel more personal, you might like to include your special interests or the things you like to do in your spare time too. How do you feel about this person? Are they someone you would like to get to know? What will you do to ensure you grow into this person?

* If you're looking for inspiration, or ideas on how to structure this, you can check out my bio in the back of this book.

A FINAL WORD FROM DOMONIQUE

Congratulations on working your way through these 8 Steps – we've covered a lot of ground and I'm proud of you for all the mindset shifts you've made and the insights you've gained, and I truly believe you are going to see some incredible shifts in the way you feel about yourself and your life because of it.

It will always be easier to have an ordinary life and, as I said right back when we started, most people are 'fine' with fine, and 'okay' with okay.

I'm so glad you're not.

I'm so glad you decided to show up and learn these simple strategies for boosting your confidence and building your self-belief.

You deserve to feel good about who you are and the life you live – not just someday, every day – and, by applying the lessons you've learned in this book, I'm confident you're well on your way.

PS

I'd love to know what your biggest insights and your favourite mindset shifts have been throughout *8 Step Confidence Crash Course.* You can find me on Instagram or Facebook @domoniquebertolucci – pop on over and say 'hello' and tell me about how you are boosting your confidence and building your self-belief.

PPS

If you never got around to downloading the free workbook created to go with this book, you can still access it for free at domoniquebertolucci.com/confidence-crash-course.

ACKNOWLEDGEMENTS

My first thanks go to my wonderful agent, Tara Wynne, for so many years and so many books. How grateful I am that you came into my life.

Thank you to Pam Brewster, Elena Callcott and all the team at Hardie Grant for embracing the Mindset Matters series and to Regine Abos for designing such gorgeous covers. To Allison Hiew, thank you for polishing my words with such care – what a delight to work with you again after all these years.

To my readers who connect with me in my Facebook group and on Instagram, thank you for sharing your experiences or simply stopping by to say hello. I put my heart and soul in my books, and it means the world to me to know that my words have reached you and perhaps even made a difference in your life.

To Holly Kahmal, your support means more to me than you will ever know, and to Lesley Brydon for reminding me who I want to be when I grow up. To Erica and Sharyn for being there since the beginning and for always showing up for yourselves.

To Mum, for your unconditional love, and unflinching presence and support. So much of who I am is not just because you've loved me but because of the way that you have demonstrated your love. And to my dad, for encouraging me to aim higher and to never accept that I was good 'for a girl'. Papa, you might not remember the first time you said that to me, but I've held your words close to my heart for more than 40 years.

To my darling Sophia and precious Toby, thank you for inspiring me with wisdom way beyond your years and for being patient with me as I locked myself away to finish this book. Lastly, to Paul, thank you for everything, always.

ABOUT THE AUTHOR

Domonique Bertolucci is the bestselling author of *The Happiness Code: Ten keys to being the best you can be* and seven other books about happiness: what it is, how to get it and, most importantly, how to keep it.

Domonique has spent the last twenty-five years working with large companies, dynamic small businesses and everyday people, teaching them how to get more happiness, more success and more time just to catch their breath.

Prior to starting her own business in 2003, Domonique worked as a model and then in the cut-throat world of high finance, where she gained a reputation as a strategic problem solver and dynamic leader. In her final corporate role, she was the most senior woman in a billion-dollar company.

Domonique's readership spans the English-speaking world, and her workshops, online courses and coach training programs are attended by people from all walks of life from all around the globe: people who want more out of life at home, at work and everywhere in between.

As well as being an accomplished professional speaker, Domonique is the host of four top-rated Audible Original Podcasts and the author of the original audiobook, *This Year Will Be Different: 8 ways to enjoy life more, regardless of what it throws at you.* She has given hundreds of interviews across all forms of media including television, radio, print and digital media; more than 10 million people have seen, read or heard her advice.

When she is not working, Domonique's favourite ways of spending her time are with her husband and two children, reading a good book and keeping up the great Italian tradition of feeding the people that you love.

Domonique jokes that she has nearly as many passports as James Bond. She is Australian by birth, Italian by blood and British by choice. She is currently based in Sydney, Australia.

OTHER BOOKS BY DOMONIQUE

MINDSET MATTERS SERIES

7 Step Mindset Makeover: Refocus your thoughts and change your life

9 Step Negativity Detox: Reset your mindset and love your life

LIFE LESSONS SERIES

The Happiness Code: 10 keys to being the best you can be

Love Your Life: 100 ways to start living the life you deserve

100 Days Happier: Daily inspiration for life-long happiness

Less is More: 101 ways to simplify your life

The Kindness Pact: 8 promises to make you feel good about who you are and the life you live

The Daily Promise: 100 ways to feel happy about your life

You've Got This: 101 ways to boost your confidence, nurture your spirit and remind yourself that everything is going to be okay

GUIDED JOURNALS BY DOMONIQUE

Live more each day: A journal to discover what really matters

Be happy each day: A journal for life-long happiness

FREE RESOURCES

You can download a range of free tools, templates and extra resources designed to help you to live your best, most brilliant life at domoniquebertolucci/com/life.

KEEP IN TOUCH WITH DOMONIQUE AT

domoniquebertolucci.com
facebook.com/domoniquebertolucci
instagram.com/domoniquebertolucci

Join Domonique's private Facebook group for regular discussion, insights and inspiration to help you get more out of life.
facebook.com/groups/domoniquebertolucci

FOR MORE INFORMATION

Find out more about Domonique's life coaching courses and programs: domoniquebertolucci.com/programs
Find out more about Domonique's training, certification, and corporate programs: domoniquebertolucci.com/training